Quantum Computing Made Easy

David Bradshaw PhD

Copyright © 2020 David Bradshaw

All rights reserved.

ISBN: 9798582264132

FOR TEAM SATALIA

CONTENTS

	Preface	vii
1	Introduction	1
2	Quantum Theory: The Basics	3
3	Qubit: The Building Block of Quantum Computing	20
4	Multiple Qubits: Quantum Circuits and Entanglement	37
5	The Quantum Computer: Its Components and Quantum Algorithms	53
6	NP-Complete Problems: Can Quantum Computers Solve Them?	67
7	Future Outlook	72
	Appendix	75
	Further Reading	77
	Glossary	79
	Biographical	95

PREFACE

This book is a product of the mutual interest that the author and the founder of Satalia, who are old high school friends, have for each other's PhD research. While David continued in academic research as a quantum physicist, Daniel Hulme created a successful computer science company that he named Satalia. It was soon realised that, surprisingly, there was a significant overlap between the two fields. This is the captivating subject known as quantum computing.

Based on the many discussions between us, the aim of this book is to explain the ideas behind quantum computing to a broad as possible audience. Quantum computing is a highly mathematical subject, but this book limits the maths – only six simplified equations are used – in favour of a set of visual representations (33 images in total) and a description of the physics behind quantum computing. Each chapter closes with a set of 'take-home messages' that summarises the text and hopefully aids the understanding of the discussed topics. The Glossary, which is towards the end of the book, should also be helpful to the reader. The book concludes with pen portraits of the scientists that contributed to the quantum physics concepts that are vital for a quantum computer.

As far as we know, an attempt to write a book on quantum computing in this manner is unique. However, our intention is to avoid the creation of a hand-waving popular-science book. Despite this we cannot claim, in any way, to be as rigorous as the textbooks in the Further Reading section of this book. Our work is far from a full course on quantum mechanics and quantum computing.

An excellent introductory course on these subjects, which has been a valuable source of knowledge, is the edX course by Professor Umesh Vazirani. When reading this book, it may comfort the reader to know that the Nobel laureate Richard Feynman once said: "I think I can safely say that nobody really understands quantum mechanics". Quantum mechanics is counter-intuitive and not something our brains are designed to fully comprehend.

We would like to dedicate this book to the past and present members of Satalia, without their extensive abilities this book would probably not exist. David is grateful for their hospitality whenever he visited Satalia's offices in London. We also thank Dr. Kayn Forbes, Dr. Garth Jones and Professor David Andrews for their helpful comments on the book, and Alex Tooth for his production of the cover and Figures 8, 10 and 11.

1 INTRODUCTION

The dictionary describes an everyday computer as "a programmable electronic device designed to accept data, perform prescribed mathematical and logical operations at high speed, and display the results of these operations". Within a computer is a microchip, which can be found in virtually every electronic device worldwide. The number of transistors on these chips has, astonishingly, increased from a few thousand in 1971 to over five billion today. In all this time, the same mathematical model for the computer has been present. But, as the size of transistors continues to get smaller and smaller, the physics that describe them will eventually enter the strange realm of quantum mechanics. This means that the previous rules, and the mathematics that go with them, may soon be overturned.

Quantum computing is a fascinating topic that combines the fields of quantum physics, information theory and computer science. A quantum computer can perform certain tasks much more quickly than any regular computer, even the greatest supercomputers. This is because quantum phenomena, which are unavailable to the everyday computer, can be implemented. Concepts such as quantum entanglement, quantum interference and superposition can produce unique computational results for certain problems.

The age of quantum computing first became a possibility when a theoretical model for a computer, based on quantum mechanics, was proposed in the early 1980s. At the time, however, researchers did not know how such a device would be constructed. Despite this, it did not deter a debate on what types of programs could run on a quantum computer. All the suggestions were considered academically interesting but impractical. The invention of Shor's algorithm in the mid-90s changed all that. This ground-breaking advance would lead to a huge up-turn in interest in quantum computing from governments, corporations and the media – which is still felt today.

This book explains quantum computing with a simple-as-possible approach. It begins, in the next chapter, with an exploration of the difference between quantum and classical mechanics and introduces the quantum ideas that were first proposed in the 1920s. The qubit, the building block of a quantum computer, and the quantum logic gates that alter them are then presented in Chapter 3; also discussed are methods for the construction of a qubit. Chapter 4 examines quantum entanglement between qubits and explains why qubits can be teleported but not copied. The five criteria for building a quantum computer, and three quantum algorithms that could run on them, are outlined in Chapter 5. The discussion on NP-complete problems, and their importance, (Chapter 6) is followed by an assessment of the latest advances in quantum computing (Chapter 7).

2 QUANTUM THEORY: THE BASICS

Quantum vs Classical Mechanics

Physics is the study of the nature and properties of matter, energy, motion and force. One branch of physics is known as classical mechanics, which is concerned with the motion of bodies under the influence of external forces – for example, gravity acting on an object. Classical mechanics has its origin in Ancient Greece, especially in the writings of Aristotle in the fourth century BCE; his purpose was to discover the principles and causes of motion, not just describe what is observed in experiment (i.e. the modern scientific method initiated by Francis Bacon in the Elizabethan era). The start of the end for the Aristotelian theory of motion began when Galileo Galilei released cannonballs and musketballs from a tall building during the Italian Renaissance – nearly two thousand years after Aristotle's original works. Sometime later, around 20 years after the Great Plague, Isaac Newton wrote his *magnum opus* "Philosophiæ Naturalis Principia Mathematica".[1] This book states his three laws of motion and became the foundation for the modern form of classical mechanics, which remained undisputed until the early 20th century. Classical mechanics was reformulated by the Italian-French mathematician Joseph-Louis Lagrange and later the Irish physicist and mathematician William Rowan Hamilton; their works are written in terms of energies, instead of forces used by Newton. While this form of mechanics correctly describes the behaviour of everyday sized objects, it fails to explain processes at very small levels. This requires the often weird and counter-

---

[1]This translates as "Mathematical Principles of Natural Philosophy". Western science at that time was almost universally written in Latin.

intuitive theory known as quantum mechanics.[2]

In classical mechanics, which is frequently termed Newtonian mechanics, identifying the state of a system means that we know the physical properties of the system (e.g. velocity, density and mass) and its future. Everything is deterministic in a classical world, once the initial conditions are established the future of the system is inevitable. For instance, when firing a projectile (a cannonball) from a cannon with a known position and inclination, the trajectory of the projectile and its landing spot can be predicted, subject to air resistance of course. In Weimar Germany in 1927, Werner Heisenberg overturned the deterministic notions of classical theory by proving that certain pairs of physical properties of a particle (which is a minuscule amount of substance) – for example, position and momentum – cannot be known simultaneously. He wrote that "the more precisely the position is determined, the less precisely the momentum is known in this instant, and *vice-versa*"; this uncertainty principle is a fundamental law of quantum mechanics, not a statement on the limitations of our current technology. Although useful in visualising his mathematically proven idea, the thought experiment known as Heisenberg's microscope (Figure 1) may lead to this misinterpretation.

---

[2]According to the correspondence principle, classical mechanics is a sub-discipline of quantum mechanics and there is no contradiction between the two subjects. However, the former is much easier to use in the study of large objects.

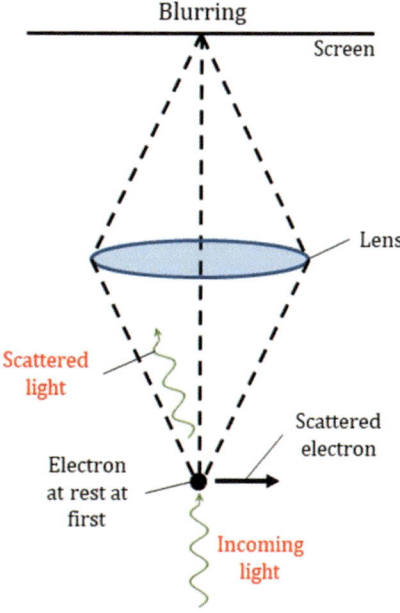

Figure 1. Visualisation of the uncertainty principle, i.e. position and momentum cannot be precisely known at the same time, with Heisenberg's microscope. An electron requires a microscope to be seen, which involves bouncing light off the electron and observing the scattered light. Unless the resolution of the microscope is extremely high, the electron will appear blurred and the position of the electron is uncertain. Finding the exact position of the electron requires a very short wavelength (high-energy) light beam. Compton scattering occurs when light strikes an electron meaning that a static electron will gain motion and, thus, momentum. The latter becomes increasingly uncertain as the energy of the light is increased. In short, if the position of the electron is known exactly then the momentum is uncertain and *vice-versa*.

Since the exact position and momentum of a particle cannot be known at the same time, the preciseness of the classical world no longer holds – i.e. the future cannot be predicted with any certainty. Quantum mechanics, as a result, involves the probability of certain events occurring. Such a probability distribution is determined from the *wavefunction* of the system, which is a mathematical abstraction that cannot be observed directly. The wavefunction is a description of the potentialities that may become realities. An actual observation or measurement – which produces the reality (as described later) – relates to only part of the probability distribution. In short, we can only find the probability that a set of predictions will actually arise. Since the motion of extremely small particles cannot be described by Newton's Laws accurately, a new set of principles based on the wavefunction are required. This was provided in the 1920s by the Austrian Erwin Schrödinger. Both his equations and his thought experiment (Schrödinger's cat) are, to this day, world-renowned.

Double-Slit Experiment

Various quantum mechanical ideas can be visualised with the Young double-slit experiment. This technique was first performed in the early 1800s by the English physician and polymath Thomas Young, over a century before any notions of quantum mechanics were ever conceived. This was a major scientific advancement at the time, but Young would not have known its vital importance to the modern understanding of the physical world. Today, his experiment is straightforward to perform with a laser beam. In fact, in his day, Young claimed that "the experiments I am about to relate ... may be repeated with great ease whenever the sun shines, and without any other apparatus than is at hand to everyone." Back then, despite mounting evidence to the contrary, Newton's 'corpuscular (particle) theory of light' was still prevalent. Until an 1818 publication by French engineer Augustin-Jean Fresnel, most scientists in those times were unconvinced by the argument that light is a wave. Fresnel's work expanded upon the experiment performed by Young, a description of the latter now follows.

If projectiles (for example, bullets from a gun) are fired in a straight line through a single slit onto a screen, the result will be a pattern of indentations that are the size and shape of the slit. In contrast, a diffraction pattern is observed on the screen when light is sent through a thin slit; meaning that the light has 'spread out' on leaving the slit, a property of a wave. If the light is sent through two parallel slits, as shown in Figure 2(a), the light is diffracted at both slits and the two 'pathways' interference with each other. This interference, another indicator of wave-like behaviour, results in a fringe pattern on the screen. In terms of light as a wave, this pattern can be explained from the fact that constructive (in-phase) and destructive (out-of-phase) interference occurs at alternating positions on the screen. So that, at certain locations, two peaks or two troughs create light of high intensity (a light fringe on the screen), while at others one trough and one peak produce no light (a dark fringe). This fringe pattern will disappear when one of the slits is blocked, since the beam is no longer split between the two slits and no interference arises.

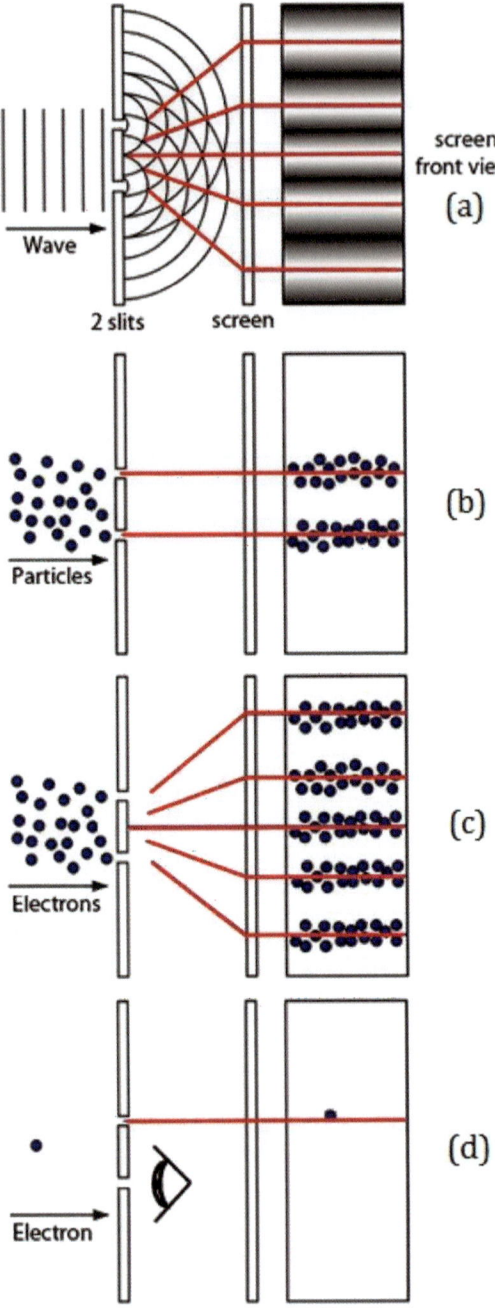

Figure 2. Depiction of the double-slit experiment, in which a beam of light (or electrons) passes through two parallel slits. (a) Interference pattern of two waves produce dark and light fringes, due to constructive and destructive interference at alternating points on the screen. (b) Everyday sized materials, such as bullets, will generate two parallel bands that mirror the two slits. (c) Extremely small particles, such as electrons, unexpectedly produce the fringe pattern that is associated with waves. (d) The fringe pattern disappears if one of the slits is blocked or the electron does not travel through it. Knowledge of the latter requires an observation, denoted by the eye symbol. Remarkably, without the observation (in-between the slits and the screen), the fringe pattern still appears when a single electron is sent through the two slits.

Following its adoption, the wave description of light remained unchallenged until 1905, when the German theoretical physicist Albert Einstein discovered that the photoelectric effect involves quanta (or discrete packets) of light energy. Under certain circumstances, light acts as a wave or a particle! This is the quantum mechanical notion of *wave-particle duality*, an insight that led to the realisation that an electron should likewise be treated as a particle or a wave. Returning to the double-slit experiment, the fringe pattern will again emerge on the screen when individual photons (quanta of light) or electrons are fired through two thin slits – as shown in Figure 2(c) – suggesting that each photon or electron travels through both slits at the same time. This contrasts with our bullets fired from a gun, which would travel through one slit or the other to produce two parallel bands on the screen, as seen in Figure 2(b). In quantum mechanics, the classical notion of a single trajectory from each slit to the screen is replaced by integration over all possible routes.[3] This is because we are dealing with the probabilities of the photon or electron striking the screen at different positions (and times); all potentialities must be considered in a *superposition*. Without an observation between the slits and the screen, the actual pathway cannot be known. Each route is considered equally probable, but the variation in phase[4] produces *quantum interference*. Analogous to the classical description, the differences in phase of each path, at varying points on the screen, generates the fringe pattern. During the Second World War, it was determined by the American theoretical physicist Richard Feynman that phase changes along each path according to its action.[5]

Feynman often used the double-slit experiment to explore a number of quantum mechanical ideas. The most intriguing is his thought experiment involving the positioning of a light detector at one of the slits, so that an observer can ascertain whether the photon passes through it or not. Since this observation determines which slit the photon travels through with complete

---

[3] Integration is required because there is an infinite number of possible trajectories. As we shall see, if the system contains finite and discrete possibilities they are simply summed.
[4] Mathematically, the phase is defined in terms of a complex number. The latter is expressed as $c + id$, where c and d are real numbers and i is an imaginary unit ($i = \sqrt{-1}$). The phase is found from $\tan^{-1}(d/c)$.
[5] A term borrowed from classical mechanics, which is defined as an integration over time of a Lagrangian (an energy). The principle of least action can be used to determine the Newtonian, Lagrangian and Hamiltonian equations of motion; it is 'least' because the path between two points requires the smallest action since, for example, light travels in a straight line.

certainty, there is zero probability that it traverses the other slit. As a result, no quantum interference occurs and the fringe pattern does not appear, as shown in Figure 2(d). This unexpected and non-deterministic process is known as the *collapse of the wavefunction*; one of the potentialities has become a reality.

Superposition and Observation

In quantum mechanics, when a particle is confined (rather than freely moving) – for instance, an orbiting electron attached to a nucleus in an atom – the system is said to be quantised, meaning that only certain quantum states are possible. In terms of our example, the electron can only occupy one of a set of quantum state possibilities (Figure 3). However, following the rules of quantum mechanics, we cannot identify which one without first making an observation.

Suppose we have a 5-state quantum system in a superposition, i.e. before the observation, with quantum states $|●⟩$, $|●⟩$, $|●⟩$, $|●⟩$ and $|●⟩$. Here, named after the English theoretical physicist Paul Dirac, the Dirac bra-ket $|·⟩$ is a representation of a quantum state. As mentioned earlier, a quantum system is described by a wavefunction – which is often symbolised by the uppercase Greek letter psi (Ψ). In our case, only 5 states are possible, so we can write;

$$\Psi = |●⟩ + |●⟩ + |●⟩ + |●⟩ + |●⟩ . \qquad (1)$$

However, in reality, some states may be more important than others. To account for this, we usually give each state a different weighting (known as the probability amplitudes, p), so that;

$$\Psi = p_\bullet|\bullet\rangle + p_\bullet|\bullet\rangle + p_\bullet|\bullet\rangle + p_\bullet|\bullet\rangle + p_\bullet|\bullet\rangle . \quad (2)$$

The wavefunction, and its weightings, is a mathematical abstraction that cannot be found by doing an experiment and, thus, can be a complex number.[6]

The probability distribution of the system – a quantity that is measurable by experiment – is found by squaring the wavefunction. Consequently, the probability of observing state $|\bullet\rangle$ is $p_\bullet^2$, $|\bullet\rangle$ is $p_\bullet^2$, $|\bullet\rangle$ is $p_\bullet^2$ and so on. When the five states are equally probable then $p_\bullet^2 = p_\bullet^2 = p_\bullet^2 = p_\bullet^2 = p_\bullet^2 = 1/5$, because adding all the squared weightings must always equal 1. This rule is known as the *normalisation condition* and it places a constraint on the possible values of the weightings.

In classical mechanics, in contrast to concepts such as Heisenberg's microscope, the act of observing a system is passive, i.e. its physical properties are unaltered by a measurement. Quantum mechanics, on the other hand, requires that any observation is an essential part of the system. This outlook requires that every possible configuration, within the known constraints, is accounted for and certain observations have a given probability of occurring. Following a measurement, the state that is observed becomes a certainty (with a probability of one) and the other 'potential' states become unattainable –

---

[6] A complex number, $c + id$, multiplied by its complex conjugate, $c - id$, gives a real number, i.e. $c^2 + d^2$. This is vital in quantum mechanics because an observable must be a real quantity; a measurement (e.g. of length) is always a number without any imaginary part.

this collapse of the wavefunction is irreversible. Therefore, following the observation of a state, the superposition 'folds' and the observed state becomes a reality at the expense of the other possibilities (Figure 4).

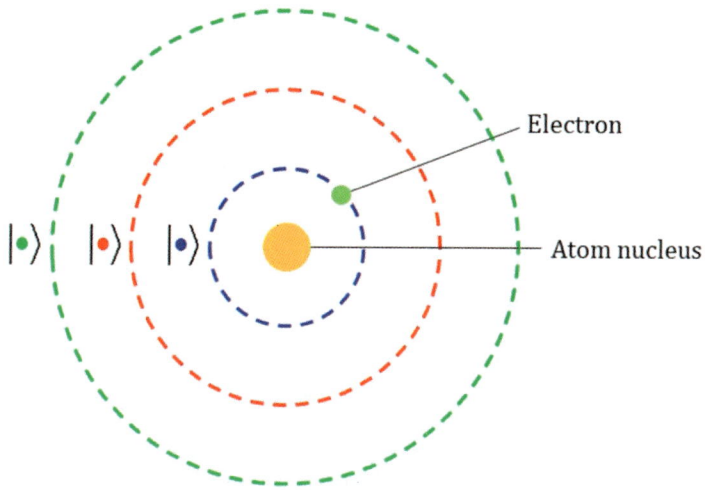

Figure 3. Representation of a 3-state quantum system based on an orbiting electron (green solid circle) bound to a nucleus (orange solid circle) in an atom. Dashed circles show the possible orbits of the electrons, which relate to quantum states $|\bullet\rangle$ (lowest orbit), $|\bullet\rangle$ (intermediate orbit) or $|\bullet\rangle$ (highest orbit). Since the electron cannot exist in-between these three orbits, the system is said to be quantised. The weighting for state $|\bullet\rangle$ is much larger than the weighting for the other states, because the electron always has a high probability of residing in the lowest orbit. However, an observation is required to discover where the electron exists for certain.

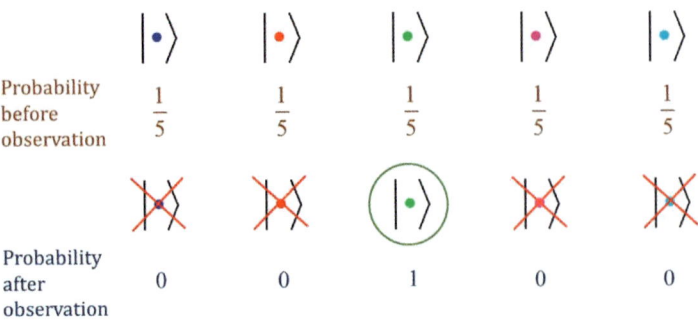

Figure 4. Probability of observing each state of a 5-state quantum system in a superposition, assuming that all the states are equally probable. Following the observation of state |●⟩, for the sake of argument, this state becomes a reality (with probability 1) at the expense of the other four potential states (all with probability 0); the latter become irreversibly unattainable. This is known as the collapse of the wavefunction, because four of its five composite states are destroyed by the observation.

EPR Paradox, Bell's Theorem and Entanglement

Until the mid-1960s, there were two prevailing perspectives on quantum mechanics: the orthodox viewpoint that the act of measurement creates the physical property, and the realist viewpoint that other information is required (called local hidden variables) for a complete description of physical reality – i.e. the characteristics of the system are defined before a measurement. Einstein was firmly in the latter camp; he devised, with two junior colleagues at Princeton, the EPR (Einstein, Podolsky and Rosen) paradox. While the original argument concerns the uncertainty principle, the American theoretical physicist David Bohm offered an experiment to test the EPR paradox; this is described as follows.

Consider the decay of a stationary neutral pion into an electron and a positron (a positively charged electron that was predicted by Dirac) that travel at great speed in opposite directions. Due to the physical law called conservation of momentum, the electron and positron must have equal and opposite quantum spins because the decayed pion had a zero spin.[7] Therefore, if the electron has an upward spin then the positron has a downward spin or *vice-versa*. Since the system is in a superposition, we cannot know which particle has an upward (or downward) spin without an observation. Suppose, when the particles are a great distance apart, that the spin of the electron is measured. Instantly, the positron will have the opposite spin (Figure 5). To a realist this is not a surprise: the particles had the observed spin when they were created, although not known to the observer. By contrast, the orthodox view that the two spins are formed by the measurement was considered preposterous by Einstein. He reasoned that this 'spooky action at a distance' cannot be instant, since a fast-than-light signal between the particles would violate special relativity (the paradox). The correlation between separate particles is now known as *quantum entanglement*.

---

[7] The concept of spin is purely quantum mechanical. It does not mean that a particle actually spins around its own axis, like a spinning top.

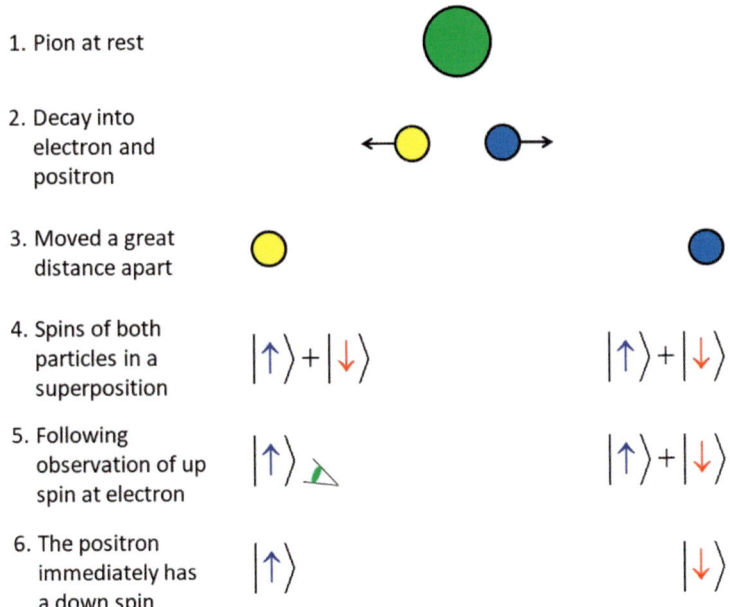

Figure 5. Illustration of quantum entanglement based on the decay of a pion (green circle) into an electron (yellow circle) and positron (blue circle).

In 1964, the Northern Irish physicist John Bell provided a new outlook on local hidden variables, which has been described as the "most profound in science". His famous theorem works on the principle that any local hidden variables (information encoded into the quantum system before observation) can be listed in every possible permutation. Returning to the EPR experiment, consider a scenario in which the entangled system contains three hidden variables and a detector (an observer) is positioned at the electron and the positron to enable the measurement of these variables. When the two detectors are oriented differently, consistent readings of the hidden variables may or may not occur – the possible permutations are given by Table 1. It does not matter which of the eight permutations actually occurs, the likelihood that the two detectors have consistent results cannot be less than ⅓. However, experiments agree with the quantum mechanical expectation (likeliest) value of ¼ – therefore, Bell's inequality fails (i.e. ¼ is less than the ⅓) proving that quantum mechanics and physical reality are not compatible with local hidden variables theory. This specific example was chosen for ease of explanation; Bell was able to prove, theoretically, that the realist viewpoint is incorrect in any circumstance. Numerous Bell test experiments have been conducted since then, all of which rule out local hidden variables.

When entangled objects are separated by great distances, they still behaviour as a single entity. This means that a measure of any single part is a measure of the whole system. One of the potentialities becomes a reality when observed, but no local hidden variables exist beforehand.

Permutation	A	B	C	AB	AC	BC	ave
1	✓	✓	✓	1	1	1	1
2	✓	✓	✗	1	0	0	⅓
3	✓	✗	✓	0	1	0	⅓
4	✗	✓	✓	0	0	1	⅓
5	✓	✗	✗	0	0	1	⅓
6	✗	✓	✗	0	1	0	⅓
7	✗	✗	✓	1	0	0	⅓
8	✗	✗	✗	1	1	1	1

Table 1. Eight possible permutations for three hidden variables (A, B and C) that are detected (denoted by a tick) or not (a cross). If the detection is consistent for two of the variables, e.g. A and B both have a tick or a cross, this is represented by 1. If the two variables are inconsistent, i.e. a cross is given for one and a tick for the other, this is signified by 0. In the final column of each permutation, the average (ave) is found by adding the three numbers and dividing by 3; this outcome is the probability that a pair has a consistent result.

Summary of Chapter 2

- Quantum mechanics is a non-deterministic theory, unlike its classical equivalent, that follows from Heisenberg's uncertainty principle

- Schrödinger's equation, rather than Newton's laws, describes a quantum system

- The double-slit experiment shows us that photons and electrons can act as waves and particles, and demonstrates quantum mechanical concepts such as superposition and collapse of the wavefunction

- Quantum systems are represented by a wavefunction in a superposition; this describes the potentialities that may become realities

- The collapse of the wavefunction occurs when the system is observed, i.e. one of the states becomes a reality at the expense of the others

- Bell's theorem rules out local hidden variables as an explanation of physical reality

3 QUBIT: THE BUILDING BLOCK OF QUANTUM COMPUTING

Qubit vs Bit

In everyday computing, a unit of data is known as a bit (shorthand for binary digit); each bit has one of two values, either 0 or 1. For a large part of the 20th century, the bit was characterised by the presence or the absence of a hole at certain positions in a punch card. In modern computing, a bit is usually based upon an electronic signal controlled by a transistor, a current (or voltage) within a cable or magnetic domains on the surface of a material. A set of eight bits is known as a byte. This form of data can be encoded into a single character, such as a letter or a symbol. It is, in terms of megabytes (10^6), gigabytes (10^9) or terabytes (10^{12}), used to define the storage capacity of random access memory and hard disk drives.

The qubit, shorthand for quantum bit, is a unit of data that has a value of 0 and 1 at the same time. A set of eight qubits is known as a qubyte. As its name suggests, qubits follow the rules of quantum mechanics – meaning that it has two states $|\bullet\rangle$ and $|\bullet\rangle$ (which represent the 0 and 1) in a superposition. The main difference between quantum computing and regular computing is the possibility of quantum entanglement and quantum interference acting between the qubits, i.e. ideas introduced in the previous chapter. As explained in detail later, quantum computers have numerous advantages over computers of the present day. However, it is important to first understand the characteristics of a single qubit; this chapter provides such an examination.

Qubits in Practice

While the understanding of the qubit is well-established, actual experimental systems to create a qubit remain challenging. Unlike bits in ordinary computers, no universal schemes for creating the qubit has been recognised. However, a large number of plausible systems have been proposed.

Any two-state quantum system is acceptable as a qubit, providing that the physical properties that represent either the 0 or 1 are distinguishable and stable. For example, the distinctive up and down spin of an electron are suitable for the two states $|\bullet\rangle$ and $|\bullet\rangle$ because a third spin configuration is not possible. In addition, approximations to two-state systems may be acceptable, i.e. multi-state schemes in which two states are sufficiently separated from each other. At present, the most promising qubit systems are those based on light, ions (charged atoms), superconductors or anyons. An outline on each is now provided.

Two-state qubits based on light can be implemented in a number of ways:

- Simply the absence and presence of a photon.

- Horizontal and vertical linearly polarised light. As depicted in Figure 6(a), light can be linearly polarised at right angles to each other.

- Left-handed and right-handed circularly polarised light. As shown in Figure 6(b), light can be circularly polarised in the clockwise (left-handed) or anti-clockwise (right-handed) direction.

- Amplitude-squeezed and phase-squeezed light. Following from Heisenberg's uncertainty principle, the number of photons (the amplitude) and the phase of a laser beam cannot both be known exactly. In squeezed light either the amplitude or the phase is made less uncertain (at the expense of the other quantity, which becomes less certain).

- Short and long paths in an interferometer (known as time-bin encoding). As portrayed in figure 6(c), light can be sent through a two-path interferometer – which splits light with mirrors and recombines them at a later stage – with pathways of different lengths.

As mentioned earlier, qubits can be based on the up and down spin of an electron and, in certain circumstances, a nucleus of an atom. Another alternative is a qubit based on charge, such as the absence and presence of an electron (a negatively charged particle). Typically, this type of system involves ions because they are larger particles and, consequently, they are much more amenable to experimental use. However, qubits constructed with superconductors are the ones currently favoured by companies such as Google, IBM, Intel and D-Wave Systems.

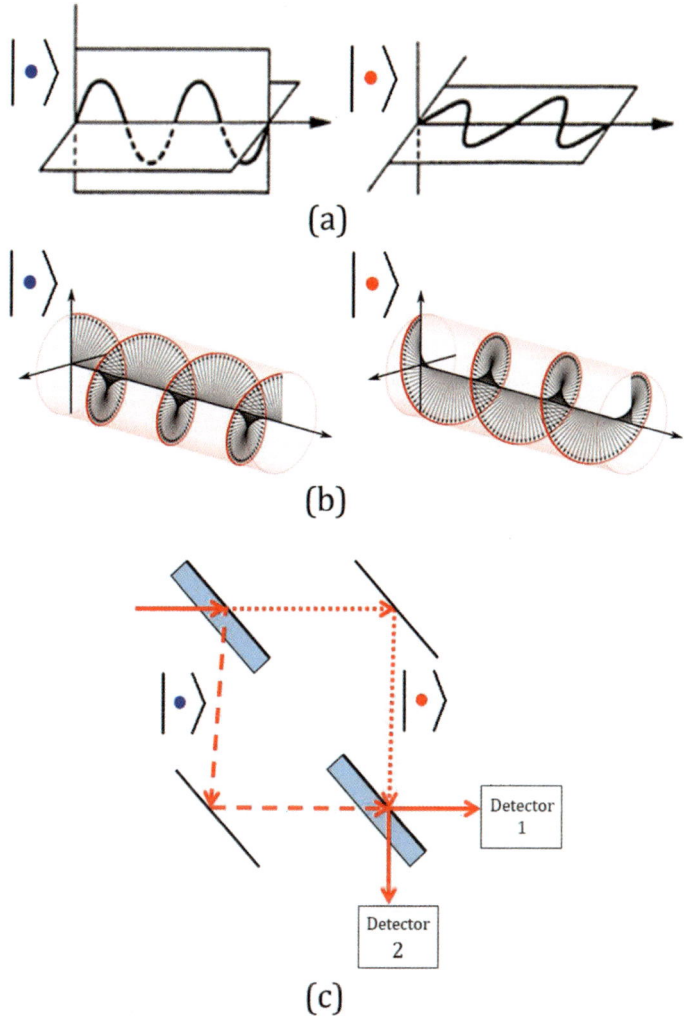

Figure 6. Qubits based on light involve: (a) linearly polarised light, in which the light is polarised in horizontal or vertical direction, (b) circularly polarised light, in which the polarisation twists clockwise or anticlockwise around a central point, or (c) an interferometer with two different pathway lengths (short and long).

A superconductor is a material that has zero electrical resistance when cooled below a certain temperature; the resistance disappears because electrons in the material bind together to create Cooper pairs that, unlike single electrons, can occupy the same space.[8] These types of qubits involve a Josephson junction, namely two superconductors separated by a thin insulating barrier, where quantum tunnelling[9] of Cooper pairs through the insulator can be observed (Figure 7):

- Charge qubits depend on the number of Cooper pairs on a superconducting island (the wire connecting an electrode of the junction to an electrode of a capacitor). This is governed by the amount of tunnelling across the junction that, due to the charge on the Cooper pairs, is controlled by an applied voltage. The states |•⟩ and |•⟩ represent the presence and absence of a substantial charge on the island, which depends on the number of Cooper pairs residing on it.

- Flux qubits work on the principle that magnetic fields are quantised inside a superconducting metal loop (an inductor). Due to this phenomenon, the states |•⟩ and |•⟩ can correspond to a clockwise and an anti-clockwise induced current in the circuit.

---

[8] More precisely, electrons are fermions with ½-spin and, therefore, cannot occupy the same space (according to the Pauli Exclusion Principle). Paired (Cooper) electrons have 0-spin or 1-spin, i.e. bosons with the ability to overlap with each other.
[9] If an energy barrier is not infinitely high, there is a very small probability that the particle can 'tunnel' or 'burrow' through the barrier. This is known as quantum tunnelling.

- Phase qubits relate to a circuit of superconducting wire that has a constant current but no voltage. In this circuit a phase difference is present across the junction.[10] This generates numerous quantum states; two of which can be used for |●⟩ and |●⟩.

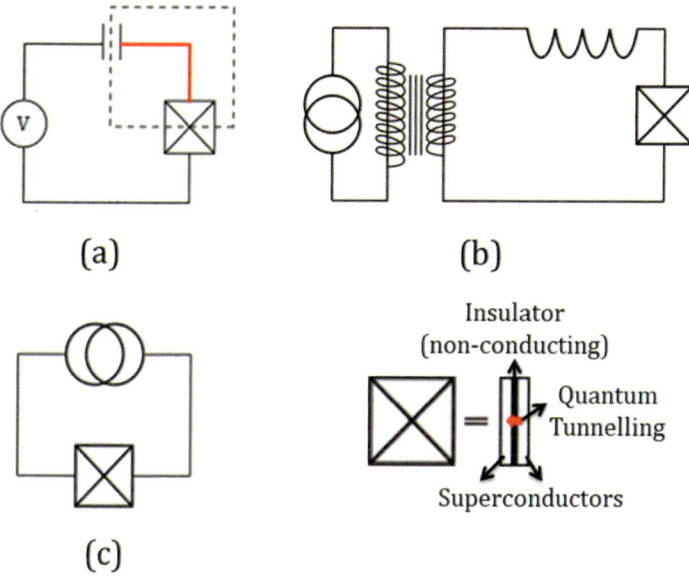

Figure 7. Superconductor qubits based on a Josephson junction (square with a cross). (a) Charge qubits involve the presence and absence of charge on a superconducting island (red line enclosed within the dashed square), which depends on quantum tunnelling of Cooper pairs through the junction; the capacitor is represented by two parallel lines and the voltmeter by a circle containing the letter V. (b) Flux qubits are based on a clockwise or an anticlockwise current in the

---

[10] It should be clearly stated, here, that the phase difference across the Josephson junction is unrelated to the idea of phase introduced elsewhere in the book.

right-hand circuit. This is produced by the combination of an inductor (the superconducting metal loop represented by a wavy line), within which only quantised magnetic fields can pass through, and the non-quantised field from the transformer (two spiral lines separated by three vertical lines); the constant current present in the left-hand circuit is denoted by the two interlocking circles. (c) Phase qubits involve a circuit with a constant current but zero voltage. In this circuit a phase difference is seen across the junction. This generates potential energy minima that contain quantised energy levels (quantum states), the two lowest are used to create qubits.

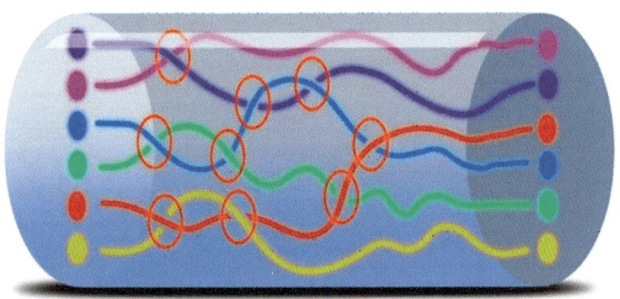

Figure 8. Anyons intertwine, by the interchange of neighbouring strands in either a clockwise or an anticlockwise direction, to form braids which are representative of quantum logic gates (red circles). Anyons remain in the sought quantum states despite small variations in their positions, meaning that topological quantum computers will be more resistant to error compared to other methods.

In contrast to the other tech giants, Microsoft is currently working on a completely different scheme known as topological quantum computing. This system is based upon anyons, string-like quasi-particles[11] that can intertwine to form braids (Figure 8). Computing of this type works on the principle that interchanging anyons, i.e. twisting strands to create braids, can generate quantum logic gates. If anyons become viable materials, topological quantum computing is expected to be more stable and error-free than any other method.

This concludes our brief discussion on potential practical systems for creating qubits; at present, in industry and academia, most attention is on the ion and the superconducting configurations.

Description of a Qubit

Thankfully, qubits are much simpler than the 5-state system we examined in Chapter 2. As we have seen, they involve two states in a superposition. Its wavefunction is thus written as;

$$\Psi = p_\bullet |\bullet\rangle + p_\bullet |\bullet\rangle, \qquad (3)$$

where the probability of observing state $|\bullet\rangle$ is $p_\bullet^2$ and state $|\bullet\rangle$ is $p_\bullet^2$. Sometimes the qubit is called a quantum coin, since only two possibilities can occur. It works using the same principles as Schrödinger's cat, in that the cat is both alive and dead – i.e. in a superposition – until

---

[11] Research on anyons is mostly mathematical but these quasi-particles have reportedly been observed in systems that use the fractional quantum Hall Effect.

an observation is made by opening the box. In the case of the qubit, this means that either |•⟩ or |•⟩ will be seen following the observation of the system. The probability of a fair quantum coin is ½ for state |•⟩ and ½ for |•⟩. While a loaded quantum coin could have a probability of ⅓ for |•⟩ and ⅔ for |•⟩, for example. These possibilities, and a third one, are shown in Figure 9. As you would expect, the two probabilities of a quantum coin always add up to 1; this is consistent with the normalisation condition, which is an important concept in quantum theory.

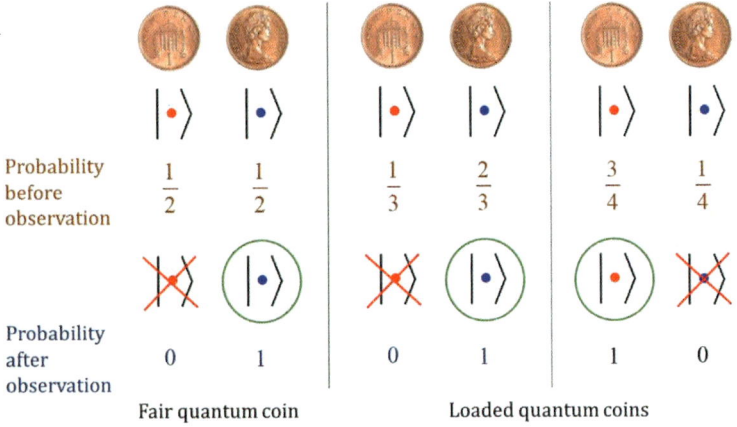

Figure 9. Diagram explaining fair and loaded quantum coins. Either |•⟩ or |•⟩ can be observed, but one of them has been chosen for clarity.

The qubit can be represented as a point on the surface of a sphere, where the North Pole represents |●⟩ and the South Pole is |●⟩. All the other positions on the surface depict a mixture of |●⟩ and |●⟩, i.e. the qubit in a superposition. If the qubit is positioned on the equator, the probably of observing |●⟩ or |●⟩ is the same; this corresponds to a fair quantum coin. A position on the Northern or Southern hemisphere means that |●⟩ or |●⟩ is more probable, respectively, which relates to a loaded quantum coin. Following an observation (a measurement), the qubit state is irreversibly positioned at the North or South Pole of the Bloch sphere.

So far the qubit has been described in terms of the states |●⟩ and |●⟩. This is known as the standard basis, it is the most frequently used basis set. However, a number of alternatives are possible; in fact, any two positions on opposite sides of the sphere can be chosen. The most common alternative is the sign basis, |+⟩ and |−⟩, in which;

$$|+\rangle = 1/\sqrt{2}\,|●\rangle + 1/\sqrt{2}\,|●\rangle,$$
$$|-\rangle = 1/\sqrt{2}\,|●\rangle - 1/\sqrt{2}\,|●\rangle. \qquad (4)$$

As shown in Figure 10, both |+⟩ and |−⟩ reside on the equator of the sphere (crucially, on opposite sides), meaning that the probability = $p_●^2 = p_●^2 = ½$ in both cases. The only dissimilarity between |+⟩ and |−⟩ is the difference in sign on the second term (the plus becomes a minus) – which is known as a phase change. The latter cannot be discovered by using the standard basis, because the probability of observing |●⟩ or |●⟩ is ½ for both |+⟩ and |−⟩ (since $1^2 = -1^2 = 1$). As a result, on this occasion, an alternative basis set should be used; the most obvious one is the sign basis itself.[12] As we will see in later chapters, the sign basis is an important tool in quantum computing.

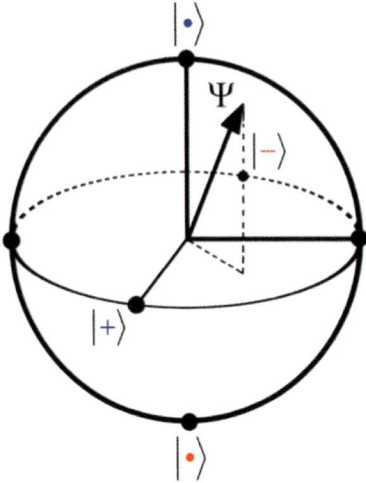

Figure 10. A Bloch sphere: a visual representation of the qubit wavefunction Ψ, which can reside at any point on the surface of the sphere. Usually the standard basis is used, |•⟩ is at the North Pole and |•⟩ at the South Pole, but the sign basis (|+⟩ and |−⟩, located at the equator) may be used instead. All the possible quantum states of the qubit can be represented on the surface of the sphere.

Single Qubit Gates

The processing of data, in the form of qubits, is a major requirement of a quantum computer. This is achieved by

---

[12] It is interesting that, relating to the uncertainty principle, in the cases when the qubit is defined in terms of |+⟩ or |−⟩ we cannot simultaneously know its exact form in terms of |•⟩ and |•⟩ (when |+⟩ or |−⟩ is observed, |•⟩ and |•⟩ are equally uncertain to the maximum extent).

using quantum logic gates,[13] the simplest of which can modify individual qubits. Since the process does not collapse the wavefunction of the qubit, the application of the quantum gate can be reversed. Visually, the logic gates change the position of the qubit on the sphere; only a combination of three logic gates is needed to access any point on the surface (Figure 11). This means that all possible quantum states of the qubit are attainable by applying quantum logic gates to them.

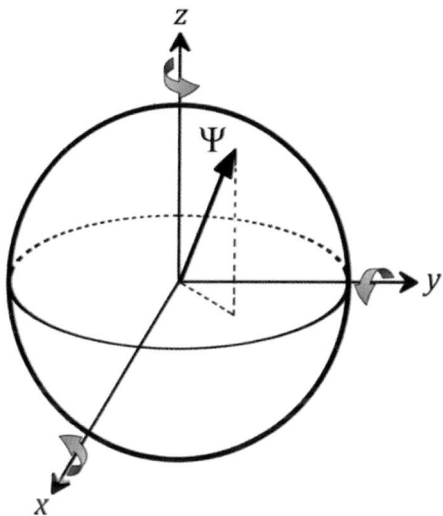

Figure 11. Quantum logic gates (represented by grey arrows) can rotate the wavefunction of the qubit around the x-, y- or z-axes. In combination, these gates allow access to any position on the surface of the Bloch sphere and, thus, all configurations of the qubit.

---

[13] Logic gates for everyday computers include AND, OR and NOT gates.

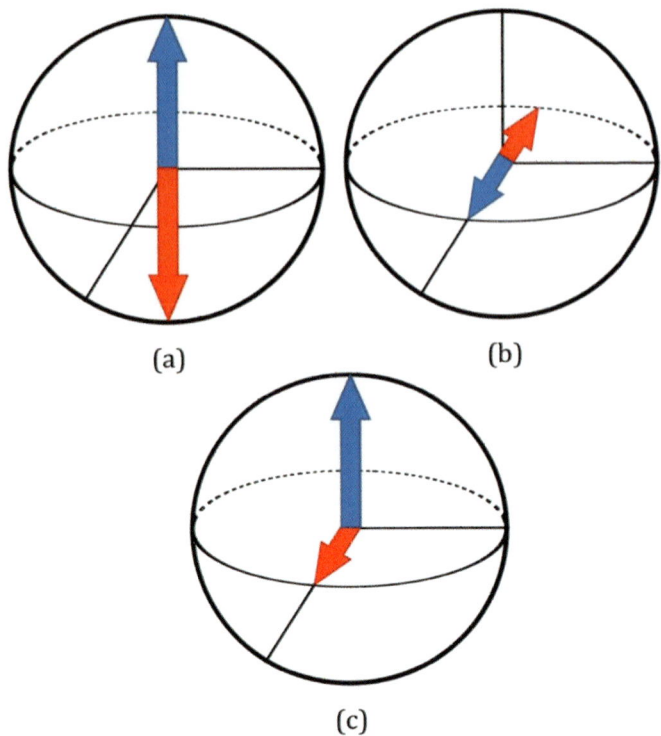

Logic Gate	Forward direction		Backward direction	
Bit Flip	$\|\bullet\rangle$	$\|\bullet\rangle$	$\|\bullet\rangle$	$\|\bullet\rangle$
Phase flip	$\|+\rangle$	$\|-\rangle$	$\|-\rangle$	$\|+\rangle$
Hadamard transform	$\|\bullet\rangle$	$\|+\rangle$	$\|+\rangle$	$\|\bullet\rangle$
	$\|\bullet\rangle$	$\|-\rangle$	$\|-\rangle$	$\|\bullet\rangle$

Figure 12. Diagrams, based on Bloch spheres, used to visualise the status of the qubit before (blue arrow) and after (red arrow) the quantum gate is applied: (a) a $|\bullet\rangle$ to $|\bullet\rangle$ bit

flip, (b) a |+⟩ to |−⟩ phase flip, (c) a |●⟩ to |+⟩ Hadamard transform. All possible transitions, when one of these three quantum logic gates acts on the standard or sign basis, are shown in the table.

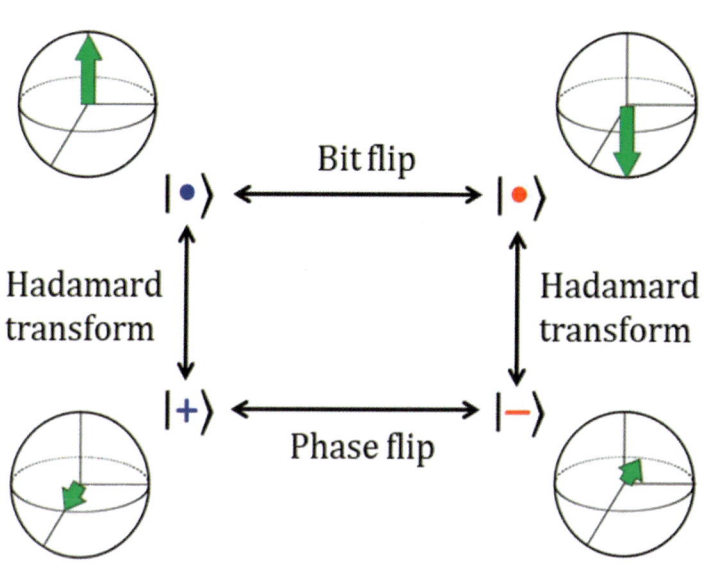

Figure 13. Inter-relationship of the quantum logic gates known as a bit flip, a phase flip and a Hadamard transform. |●⟩ and |●⟩ relate to the standard basis, |+⟩ and |−⟩ to the sign basis.

Quantum gates of special interest are called a bit flip, a phase flip and a Hadamard transform. As shown in Figure 12(a)-(c), the bit flip transforms |●⟩ into |●⟩ or *vice-versa*,[14] the phase flip interchanges the phase (for example, |+⟩ becomes |−⟩) and the Hadamard gate

---

[14] The bit flip is a quantum gate analogous to the NOT gate.

converts the standard basis ($|\bullet\rangle$ and $|\bullet\rangle$) into the sign basis ($|+\rangle$ and $|-\rangle$) or the converse. The Hadamard transform can, thus, split a single state into two states in a superposition. All three gates are interrelated, as defined in Figure 13. In the next chapter, quantum logic gates that manipulate multiple qubits are introduced.

Summary of Chapter 3

- Rather than the bits of conventional computers, the building blocks of a quantum computer are qubits

- While a bit is a zero *or* a one, a qubit is a zero *and* a one in superposition

- Any two-state quantum system is acceptable as a qubit, providing that the physical properties that represent either the 0 or 1 are distinguishable and stable

- A practical qubit system could be made with light, ions, superconductors or anyons

- The qubit can be visualised as a point on the surface of a sphere

- Qubits are usually defined in a standard basis, i.e. with $|\bullet\rangle$ and $|\bullet\rangle$, but sometimes it is beneficial to use the sign basis, symbolised by $|+\rangle$ and $|-\rangle$

- The processing of data, in the form of qubits, is accomplished by using quantum logic gates

- The bit flip transforms $|\bullet\rangle$ into $|\bullet\rangle$, the phase flip converts $|+\rangle$ into $|-\rangle$

- The Hadamard gate interchanges the qubit from the standard basis to the sign basis

- A Hadamard transform can split a single state into two states in a superposition

4 MULTIPLE QUBITS: QUANTUM CIRCUITS AND ENTANGLEMENT

Reversible Logic Gates

Quantum logic gates are always reversible, unlike most logic gates in ordinary computers. However, reversible gates have interested computer scientists for decades, well before any serious thought of building a quantum computer. The appeal arose since reversible gates enable reduced heat dissipation, which promotes faster computer processing speeds. In 1961, the German-American physicist Rolf Landauer linked this irreversibility, and subsequent data loss, with an unsought discharge of energy; this means that any data losses at a logic gate produce heat. For example, if two 0s are input into an AND logic gate then the output will be a 0. But when the AND gate is applied again the two 0s *may* not be returned, since two other outcomes are possible; this is shown in Figure 14(a). As a result, AND gates are irreversible and create a loss of data. In contrast, the NOT gate is reversible since, as depicted Figure 14(b), an input of 0 into a NOT gate gives an output of 1 and applying the NOT gate again returns the 0. The quantum logic gates of the previous chapter also have reversibility. If the bit flip, phase flip or Hadamard transform is applied twice the original qubit is returned, i.e. the qubit moves to a different position on the sphere surface at first but then returns to its original position following the second application.

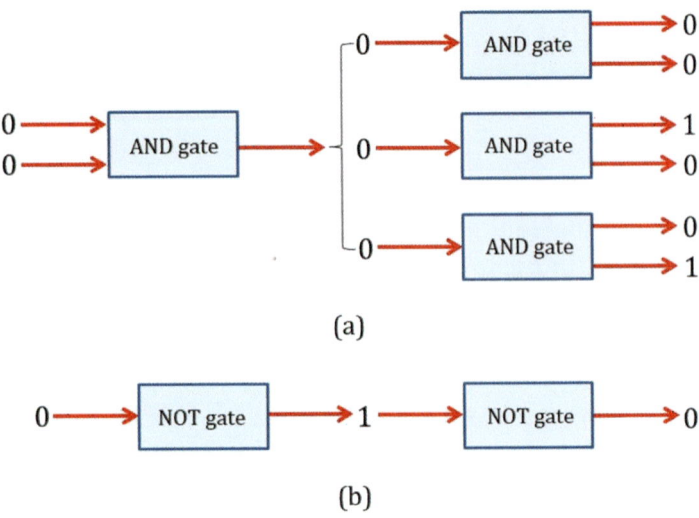

Figure 14. (a) When 0 and 0 (alternatively written [0,0]) are input into an AND gate, the output is 0. When 0 is input into an AND gate there is three possible outputs [0,0], [0,1], [1,0]. As a result, the AND gate is irreversible since the two input 0s may not be returned. It should be noted that this is an oversimplification for ease of explanation, AND gates have two inputs and one output (which automatically makes them irreversible). (b) Using the same reasoning, the NOT gate is reversible since the 0 becomes a 1 on its first application and the 0 is returned on its second use. The first process (0→1) can be reversed (1→0).

It is impossible to have a reversible AND gate with only two inputs, which means that a gate of this type is more complicated to construct. Typically, they are based on a Toffoli gate[15] which requires three output bits (each with either a 0 or a 1) and the input of two control bits and a

---

[15] An alternative reversible AND gate uses a Fredkin gate.

target bit. In fact, all reversible gates have the same number of inputs and outputs. Figure 15 is a representation of the Toffoli gate: the two control bits (A and B) are unaltered by the gate, while the target bit (C) interchanges when A and B are both 1. For example, inputting A = 1, B = 1, C = 1 into a Toffoli gate returns A = 1, B = 1, C = 0. Reversible gates do not lose data, only move it around; excess energy, in the form of heat, is therefore *not* lost to the surroundings. Unlike a simple AND gate, a Toffoli gate can be used in a quantum computer because its reversible characteristics are consistent with a quantum logic gate.

Quantum Circuits

In upcoming text, we will examine important quantum computing circuits and how, in certain circumstances, they can achieve results inconceivable with present day computing. At this point, it seems appropriate to briefly outline the characteristics of a quantum circuit.

Having a similar appearance to the classical circuit of Figure 15, quantum circuits are a set of wires (horizontal lines) that carry qubits to and from quantum logic gates (rectangular blocks) that can modify them. We imagine the qubits moving through the wires from left to right. Because of their quantum nature, these circuits are reversible meaning that the number of input qubits is matched by the number of outputs. Some of these outputs may be useless and presumed to be garbage,[16]

---

[16] A garbage qubit may prevent quantum inference and produce unwanted results. Unfortunately, they cannot be simply 'thrown away' because they are entangled to the other qubits. One way to remove them is by observation, but this is very unhelpful because

but they are needed for reversibility reasons. When an observation or measurement is made, the superposition of the qubit is lost and the result acts like a classical bit; this 'bit' is represented by a double line and any measurement (read-out) is depicted by an image of a meter.

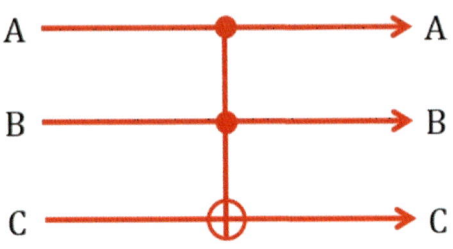

Input			Output		
A	B	C	A	B	C
0	0	0	0	0	0
0	0	1	0	0	1
0	1	0	0	1	0
0	1	1	0	1	1
1	0	0	1	0	0
1	0	1	1	0	1
1	1	0	1	1	1
1	1	1	1	1	0

Figure 15. Depiction of the Toffoli gate, where A, B and C are either a 0 or a 1. The red dot signifies that the control bits A and B do not change, the symbol ⊕ means the target bit C only interchanges (i.e. from 0 to 1 or *vice-versa*) when A and B are both 1. All possible combinations are shown in the table.

---

the wavefunction for all the qubits would then collapse. A viable method to counter this problem is to reverse the applied quantum logic gates, but retrieve the wanted qubits before this reversal is applied.

The simplest quantum circuit contains a single qubit gate; an example, involving a Hadamard transform, is presented in Figure 16. Complexities may arise, because of quantum entanglement, when multiple qubits are input into the circuit. A discussion on this subject is provided in the next section. A quantum logic gate that acts on two qubits at once to create an entangled state is introduced afterwards.

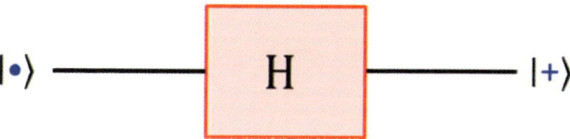

Figure 16. A quantum circuit involving a Hadamard transform, H: the wire (horizontal line) transports the qubit with state |●⟩ to the Hadamard transform gate (rectangular block) that converts it into |+⟩.

Entangled Qubits

The phenomenon of quantum entanglement, which is introduced in Chapter 2, is vital to the operation of a quantum computer. Firstly, let us examine the wavefunction of two independent qubits with no entanglement. This is found by multiplying the wavefunction of the first qubit – given by equation (3) – with that of the second. So that, if both qubits are fair quantum coins, we find;

$$\Psi = (1/\sqrt{2}\,|●⟩ + 1/\sqrt{2}\,|●⟩)(1/\sqrt{2}\,|●⟩ + 1/\sqrt{2}\,|●⟩)$$
$$\Psi = ½\,|●●⟩ + ½\,|●●⟩ + ½\,|●●⟩ + ½\,|●●⟩, \quad (5)$$

where |••⟩ is a quantum state in which the first and second dots correspond to the first and second qubits, respectively. The probability of observing each of these four states (either |••⟩, |••⟩, |••⟩ or |••⟩)) is ¼, which is consistent with the normalisation condition.

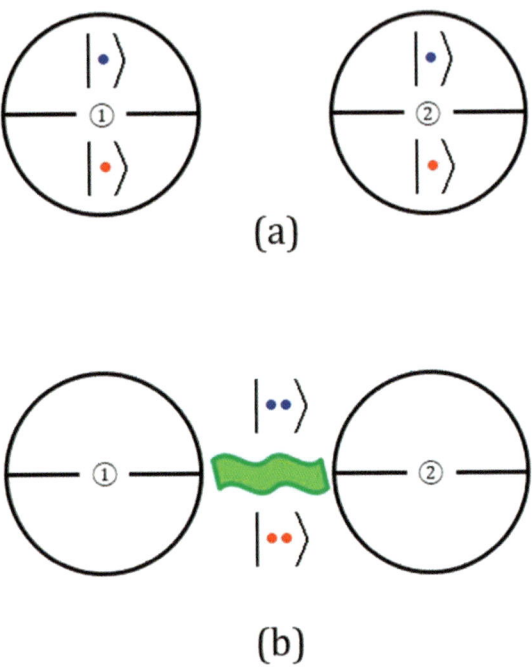

Figure 17. Two qubits that are (a) independent and (b) entangled (depicted by the green wave line); ① labels the first qubit and ② the second qubit. The entangled states |••⟩ and |••⟩ cannot be decomposed into |•⟩ and |•⟩ meaning that the qubits in (b) cannot be treated as separate entities.

In contrast, entangled qubits are totally inter-twined and cannot be treated as individual, isolated entities. A diagram representing the difference between entangled and independent qubits is given in Figure 17(a)-(b). Unlike equation (5), entangled quantum states cannot be expressed within parentheses. The simplest example of a state for entangled qubits is known as a Bell state (named after John Bell), which is written as;

$$\Psi = 1/\sqrt{2}\,|\bullet\bullet\rangle + 1/\sqrt{2}\,|\bullet\bullet\rangle. \qquad (6)$$

Here, following observation of the first qubit, which collapses the wavefunction of the entangled qubits, the state of the first qubit is either $|\bullet\rangle$ or $|\bullet\rangle$ (both have a probability of ½). As shown in Figure 18, when the first qubit is observed to have the state $|\bullet\rangle$ or $|\bullet\rangle$ then the second qubit becomes $|\bullet\rangle$ or $|\bullet\rangle$, respectively. To be clear, although the observation occurs at the first qubit, the superposition state of the second qubit is also instantly lost. While no other outcome is possible for the Bell state, more complicated entangled states may still have residual entangled states after the observation of a qubit. An example of this is given in Figure 19.

We now introduce a quantum circuit that converts two independent qubits into an entangled Bell state (Figure 20). This circuit contains a Hadamard transform and a controlled-NOT gate. The latter is simply a Toffoli gate with one (rather than two) control qubit; when this control is $|\bullet\rangle$, the target qubit interchanges from $|\bullet\rangle$ to $|\bullet\rangle$ or *vice-versa*.

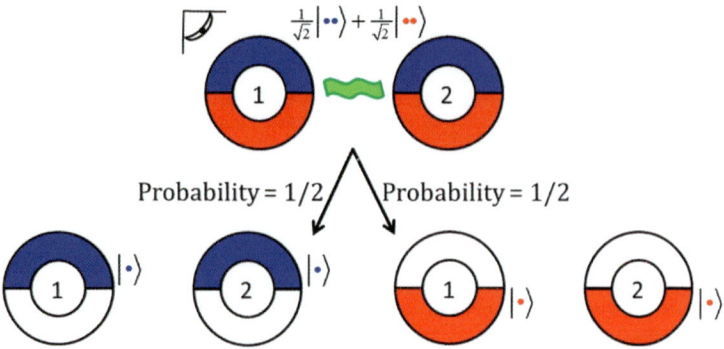

Figure 18. Flowchart showing the effect of an observation on two entangled qubits in a Bell state. After observation (the eye) of the first qubit, the wavefunction collapses and only one quantum state of the first qubit remains; there is a 50:50 chance of it being $|\bullet\rangle$ or $|\bullet\rangle$. Since the qubits are entangled, the second qubit also loses its superposition; it will always match the new state of the first qubit in this case.

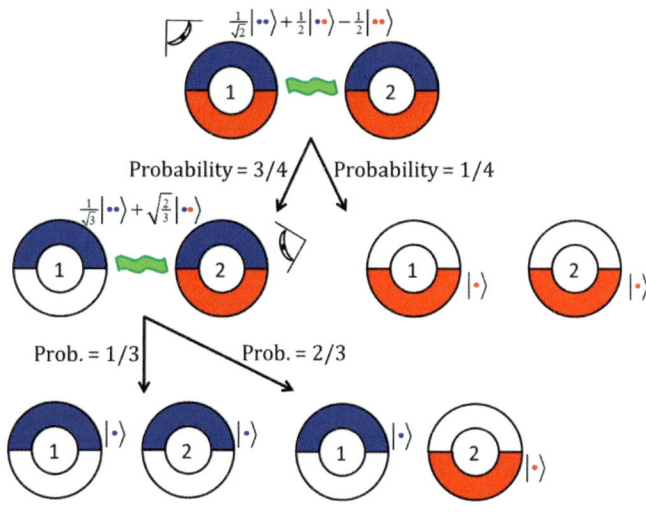

Figure 19. Flowchart showing the effect of observations on two entangled qubits, in a case where a residual entangled state persists following observation of the first qubit.

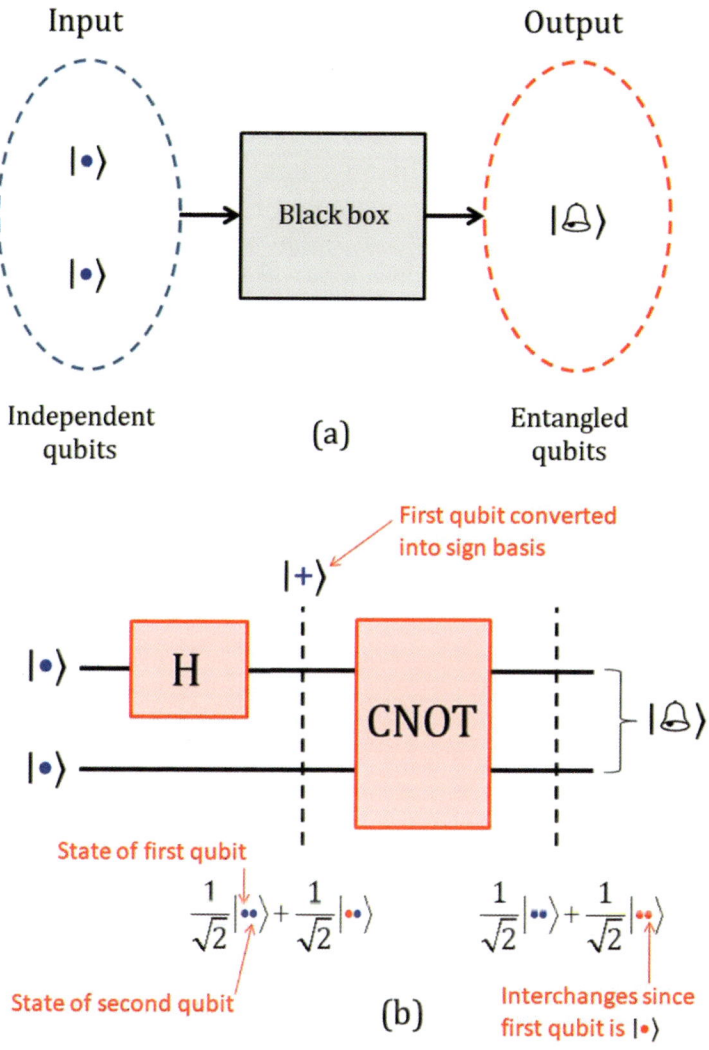

Figure 20. (a) Black box representation (i.e. the internal workings are missing) for the entanglement of two independent qubits, $|\bullet\rangle$, into a Bell state. (b) Quantum circuit to achieve this entanglement with a Hadamard transform (H) and a controlled-NOT gate (CNOT). The state of the two qubits is provided at certain positions (at vertical dashed lines).

No-Cloning Principle and Quantum Teleportation

In everyday computing, it is vital that bits can be copied and transferred to other positions – for instance, in the memory – with ease. Ideally, in terms of qubits, this ability should be present in a quantum computer. But, in reality, a qubit cannot be copied or cloned. This is disappointing because irretrievable data loss occurs when the irreversible observation is made; meaning that all the information connected to the state $|\bullet\rangle$ disappears when $|\bullet\rangle$ is observed or *vice-versa*. The simple solution to this problem is to copy the unknown (unobserved) qubit several times and then observe each clone individually to determine the lost information. The no-cloning principle (Figure 21) scuppers this proposal. The closest alternative is quantum teleportation, i.e. the transmission of an unknown qubit from one position to another, in which the original qubit is destroyed. This complicated procedure is now outlined with the tools we have developed so far.

Figure 21. Cloning of an unknown qubit, so that it is replicated and a state $|\bullet\rangle$ is converted into it, by a quantum logic gate is impossible. This is known as the no-cloning principle.

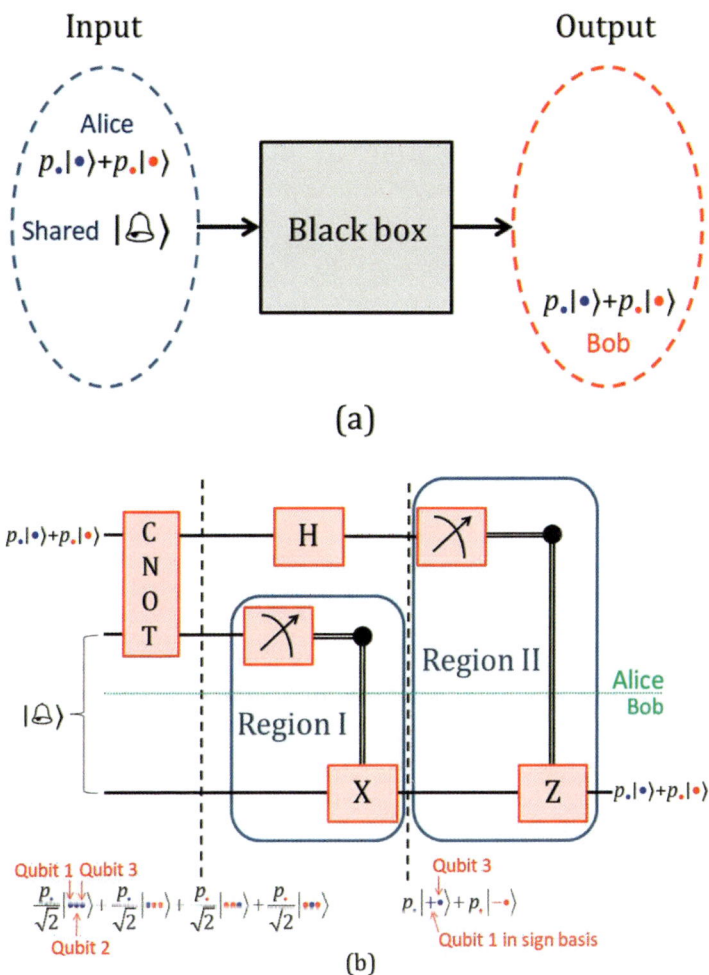

Figure 22. (a) Black box representation for quantum teleportation. Alice sends an unknown qubit to Bob. To enable this transfer, Alice and Bob each have an entangled qubit in a Bell state. (b) A quantum circuit for quantum teleportation. Two qubits are held by Alice (appearing above the green dotted line), the first is the unknown qubit to be

transferred; the third one (below the dotted line) is held by Bob. The H, X and Z gates are a Hadamard transform, a bit flip and a phase flip, respectively; the meter symbol denotes an observation. Following the controlled-NOT gate, the state of the qubits is expressed at the lower left and given again after Region I. The details on Region I and II are presented in Figures 23 and 24, respectively. The unknown qubit is reproduced by Bob at the end of the circuit.

In the field of quantum information, it is convention that data sharing involves two people named Alice and Bob. To begin, as shown in Figure 22(a), Alice has an unknown qubit that she wants to send to Bob and a second qubit that is entangled to a third one held by Bob. Looking at the quantum circuit of Figure 22(b), a controlled-NOT gate is first applied to Alice's two qubits. Then, on entering Region I, Alice measures her entangled qubit and sends the outcome to Bob. If the result is $|\bullet\rangle$ Bob does nothing, otherwise he applies a bit flip to his qubit (Figure 23). At this point in the circuit, Alice applies a Hadamard transform to the unknown qubit, takes a measurement and the result is again transmitted to Bob. If the outcome is $|\bullet\rangle$ Bob does nothing, otherwise he applies a phase flip (Figure 24). After region II, Bob has re-created the unknown qubit and Alice has destroyed both her qubits due to their observation. The latter means that quantum teleportation is entirely compatible with the no-cloning principle. To summarise, a qubit cannot be copied before its observation, but it can be transported from one location to another.

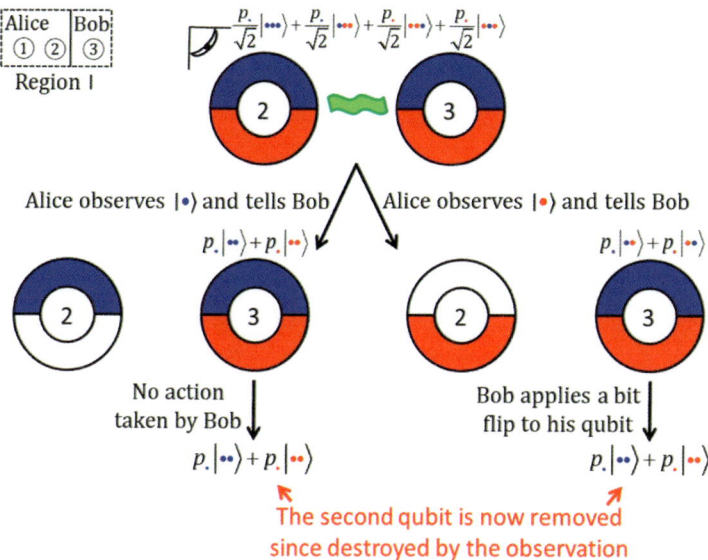

Figure 23. The effect of the observation of Alice's entangled qubit in Region I. Inset: Alice holds qubits 1 (unaltered in Region I, so it does not appear in the flowchart) and 2, Bob has qubit 3. Alice observes qubit 2 and sends the result to Bob. If the result is $|\bullet\rangle$ Bob does nothing, if $|\bullet\rangle$ he applies a bit flip on qubit 3. The state of the qubits on entering and leaving Region I are given; the output state is the same whichever route is taken.

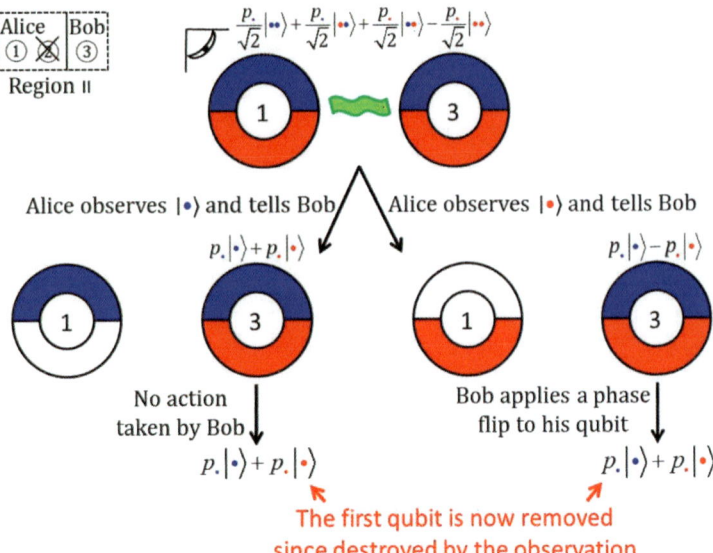

Figure 24. The effect of the observation of Alice's qubit 1 in Region II. Alice observes her qubit and sends the result to Bob. If the result is $|\bullet\rangle$ Bob does nothing, if $|\bullet\rangle$ he applies a phase flip on qubit 3. The output is Bob's recreation of the unknown qubit that was initially held by Alice.

Summary of Chapter 4

- Quantum logic gates are reversible, while most logic gates in ordinary computers are not

- Toffoli gates are reversible AND gates that can be used in quantum computing

- Quantum circuits are a set of wires that carry qubits to and from quantum logic gates that modify them

- Quantum circuits have the same number of input and output qubits

- Quantum entanglement is vital to the operation of a quantum computer

- Entangled qubits are totally inter-twined and cannot be treated as individual, isolated entities

- Observation of an entangled qubit affects all the qubits its entangled to. This is an irreversible event

- The simplest example of a quantum state for entangled qubits is a Bell state

- A quantum circuit, containing a Hadamard transform and a controlled-NOT gate, can create a Bell state from two independent qubits

- A qubit cannot be copied before its observation. This is known as the no-cloning principle

- With a complicated quantum circuit, a qubit can be transferred from one position to another. This is known as quantum teleportation

5 THE QUANTUM COMPUTER: ITS COMPONENTS AND QUANTUM ALGORITHMS

DiVincenzo's Criteria

In the previous chapter, we looked at quantum circuits with a limited number of input and output qubits. When more qubits are added to create a quantum computer there is an exponential growth in data. This means that, when around 500 qubits are present, there is seemingly more data available than the number of particles in the universe. The problem is that, following an observation, almost all of this data is lost. Only the information connected to the observed state is found (Figure 25). The remaining gigantic dataset cannot be replicated (due to the no-cloning principle) and, thus, saved from extinction. Despite this inevitable data loss, the role of a quantum computer is to manipulate the unseen data before any observation is made – so that unique and previously unattainable results can be obtained. This means that the observation should be the final step in the quantum computing process. A workable device should not collapse the wavefunction of the qubits until this point.

A quantum computer, i.e. a programmable quantum information processing device, performs tasks by modifying a set of labelled qubits in a quantum register. This is represented by quantum circuits that contain quantum logic gates. They differ to electronic circuits in everyday computers because phenomena such as quantum entanglement and quantum interference can be exploited in them. Quantum computers can perform both everyday computing tasks and the quantum mechanical processing of qubits. However, unless quantum algorithms are used – such as the ones introduced later in this chapter – no quantum results are attainable; if a quantum computer is not running a quantum algorithm, it is no different to a regular computer.

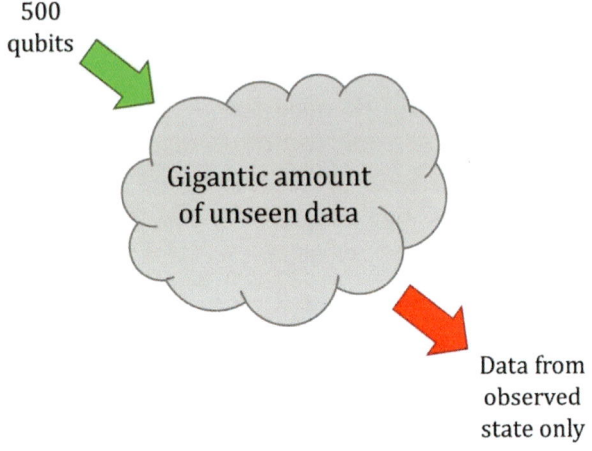

Figure 25. Cartoon showing that an observation destroys a huge amount of unseen data.

The five criteria for building a quantum computer were proposed by the theoretical physicist David DiVincenzo in 2000. These are:

1. Start the system in a well-defined and stable quantum state [Practical systems to achieve this is outlined in Chapter 3]
2. Must have a sufficiently large number of individually addressable qubits [A way to order

qubits, so that they can be labelled, is given in the Appendix]
3. Feasible to apply quantum logic gates to each qubit or set of qubits [Quantum gates are discussed in Chapters 3 and 4]
4. Preservation of qubits in the quantum registry for a large number of operations [This means limiting the quantum decoherence, which is discussed in the next section].
5. Possible to read-out the quantum state of each qubit with high fidelity [This is the observation that collapses the wavefunction of the qubits].

Research on all five criteria has greatly advanced in the last 30-40 years. However, present day quantum registers are still limited to a few or 10s of qubits. While a viable quantum computer requires several hundred or thousands of qubits. A major cause of this limitation is the effect known as quantum de-coherence, the subject of the next section.

Quantum Decoherence

Despite the research advancements at the time (see below), a viable quantum computer was still considered improbable in the mid-90s. This is because quantum systems are notoriously fragile, which means that their quantum characteristics are easily lost. In terms of quantum computing, this loss or decoherence originates from the interaction of the qubits with their surroundings. This has the same effect as an observation.

Quantum decoherence is probably the biggest hurdle to overcome when constructing a quantum computer. It represents a decay of the data encoded into the quantum register, so that errors continually arise. Unfortunately, this decay grows as the number of qubits increase. Consequently, the viability of a quantum computer is compromised. It is, therefore, vital to develop a strategy to reduce the effects of quantum decoherence. The recent developments in error correction techniques have helped achieve this aim.

In everyday computing, error correction – the reconstruction of corrupted data – is achieved by data copying. However, the no-cloning principle excludes this possibility in a quantum computer. Luckily, however, techniques already available for regular computing can, surprisingly, be modified to create sophisticated quantum error correction techniques. Primarily, they involve encoding the data into additional qubits, which then check for and eliminate various types of error. This vast subject has become one of the most extensively developed areas of quantum computing.

These error correction techniques, combined with fault-tolerant procedures, make a robust quantum computer a possibility in the not-too-distant future. However, such a device cannot produce unique results without a set of quantum algorithms to run on them; this is the topic of the next sections.

Simon's algorithm

Algorithms are list of instructions, given to a computer, that are used to solve a problem. They typically involve many repetitions of the same task with a large number of inputs. Quantum algorithms can produce solutions – for certain problems – vastly more rapidly than ordinary algorithms. This is known in computer science as speed-up. For the rest of this chapter, we will examine quantum algorithms. A proper explanation is heavily mathematical. So, to circumvent these intricacies, we offer an over-simplified taster of the ideas behind them.

Although they have little practical value, early quantum algorithms proved that certain problems can be solved much faster than standard algorithms. One of these processes is known as Simon's algorithm – which will now be explained. There is a string (a sequence of numbers, labelled x) input into a black box, i.e. where the internal workings are missing, with an output $f(x)$; this is shown in Figure 26. For simplicity, we will presume that the string has three numbers. Let us also assume that the output is the same for two of the input strings, so that $f(x) = f(x+s)$ – it is the string, s, that Simon's algorithm will find.

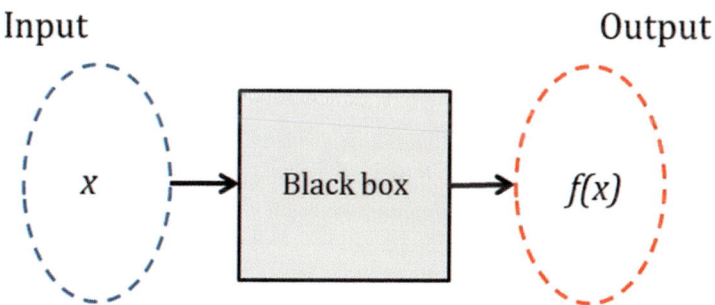

Figure 26. Simon's algorithm is based upon the input of a string x (a sequence of numbers) into a black box that will output a string $f(x)$, which is technically called the function of x.

For ease of understanding, we will now look at the example given in Table 2: the first column provides all the possible combinations for a three-digit string, only using 0s and 1s, and the second column is the example outputs. We can see that the 000 and 101, 001 and 100, 010 and 111, 011 and 110 pairs give the same output; looking at the first pair it is clear that $s = 101$ (i.e. 101 - 000). For this specific example, the numbers in the string s are easy to find. Simon's algorithm discovers a solution for any possible input string of any length.

Since quantum algorithms can be represented by a sequence of quantum gates, Simon's algorithm can be depicted by Figure 27. The important parts of this quantum circuit are:

1. Point A, the input qubits with state $|\bullet\rangle$ are converted into x.
2. Point B, the black box converts x into $f(x)$, which is then observed at Point C. This observation means that only one of the four pairs in Table 2 (in the example case) still exists.
3. The remaining two states are in a superposition and contain the string s. The latter, which is the solution of the problem, can be calculated after another observation at Point C.

Simon's algorithm could be understood as a double-slit experiment (introduced in Chapter 2), where the first observation creates two states that act as the two slits. The output of the circuit is a set of results (fringes) that appear due to quantum interference. It is from the observation of these 'fringes' that the string s is found.

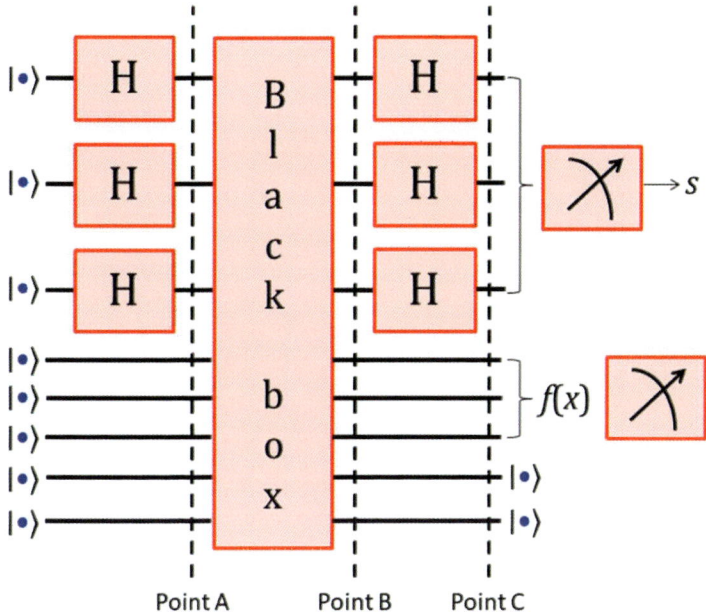

Figure 27. The quantum circuit for Simon's algorithm.

An algorithm on a regular computer would require the input of random strings until the same output is found for two of them. This is an extremely slow process for long strings (i.e. those with lots of numbers), which computer scientists call exponential time. In contrast, Simon's algorithm works in the vastly quicker polynomial time.

x	f(x)
000	000
001	010
010	001
011	100
100	010
101	000
110	100
111	001

Table 2. Example outputs (second column) for the eight possible combinations of an input string with three numbers. The rows with identical colours have the same output. From the corresponding input pairs (000 and 101, for example) the target string, *s*, can be identified.

Shor's Algorithm

Inspired by Simon's algorithm, the first quantum algorithm that could truly produce revolutionary results on a quantum computer was invented by the American mathematician Peter Shor in 1994. Known as Shor's algorithm, its aim is to efficiently factorise integers (loosely, the opposite of multiplying numbers; for example, the integer 21 can be factorised into 7 and 3). It is difficult for a regular algorithm to do this efficiently for very large numbers, which is exploited by the cryptography schemes used in internet security protocols. Shor's algorithm proved that such encryption measures could be quickly broken on a viable quantum computer. At the time, this possibility generated much excitement; it catalysed widespread interest in quantum computing, especially from industry and government.

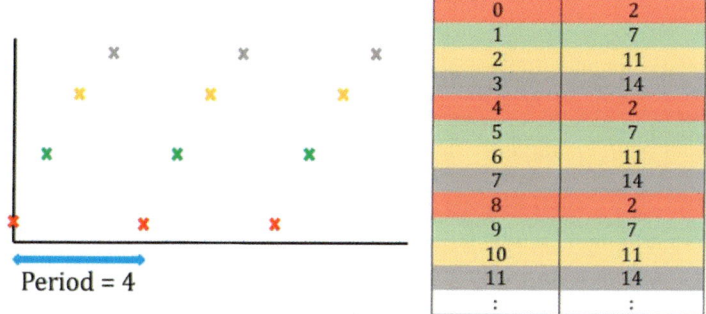

Figure 28. Graph showing a set of example results (plotted using the numbers in the Table) that continually repeat themselves; they have a period of 4. The rows in the table with identical colours have the same output. This is a simple example that is comparable to Table 2; Shor's algorithm can find the period for huge input numbers.

Instead of pursuing the string s, Shor's algorithm searches for the period of a set of results that continually repeat themselves (Figure 28). With this knowledge the correct factors are quickly discovered. The quantum circuit of Shor's algorithm has a similar look to Figure 27. The main differences are the Hadamard transforms are replaced by quantum Fourier transforms[17] and a set of

---

[17] A Hadamard transform is a special case of a quantum Fourier transform.

states remain after the first observation, instead of the two states of Simon's algorithm. Due to the latter, Shor's algorithm is comparable to a multiple-slit experiment.

Grover's Algorithm

Devised by the Indian-American computer scientist Lov Grover in 1996, Grover's algorithm is the most famous quantum algorithm after Shor's algorithm. While the latter focusses on a narrow (but important) range of problems, Grover's algorithm can be applied to an extensive set of problems.[18] The most well-known is the needle-in-a-haystack problem which, with a regular algorithm, involves examining each piece of data (the 'hay') one-by-one until the sought data (the 'needle') is discovered.[19] As you can imagine, for an enormous dataset this is inefficient and very time consuming.

Suppose we search a huge unstructured database for a single piece of data, which is defined as x^* (Figure 29). In this scenario, the previous tactic of creating a set of states via an observation cannot occur and, thus, there is *no* speed-up compared to an ordinary algorithm in such a set-up. This means that a different strategy is required,

---

[18] However, Grover's algorithm has only a quadratic speed-up compared to a regular algorithm. This is slower than the exponential speed-up of Simon's algorithm and Shor's algorithm.

[19] In terms of computer science, this problem involves searching unordered arrays in a database. When searching ordered arrays, quantum algorithms have no significant advantage over regular algorithms.

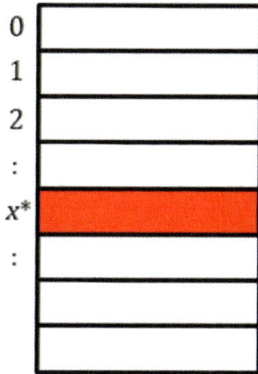

Figure 29. Representation of the needle-in-a-haystack problem. The task is to find a single piece of data, x^*, in an unstructured database containing an enormous amount of data.

one which is based upon a phase inversion and a reflection around the average (Figure 30). The vital parts of the quantum circuit for Grover's algorithm (Figure 31) are as follows:

1. Point A, the input qubits with state |•⟩ are converted into x.
2. Point B, black box 1 converts x into $f(x)$. The latter equals 1 for x^* only, when this happens the sign on |−⟩ interchanges and then the 'needle' (but nothing else) undergoes phase inversion.
3. Point C, black box 2 reflects everything around the average position.
4. The phase inversion and the reflection around the mean are continually repeated.

The final step eventually creates a probability of ½ that x^* is observed.[20] So there is a 50:50 chance of observing the 'needle' when an observation is made; if it is not seen the whole process is repeated.

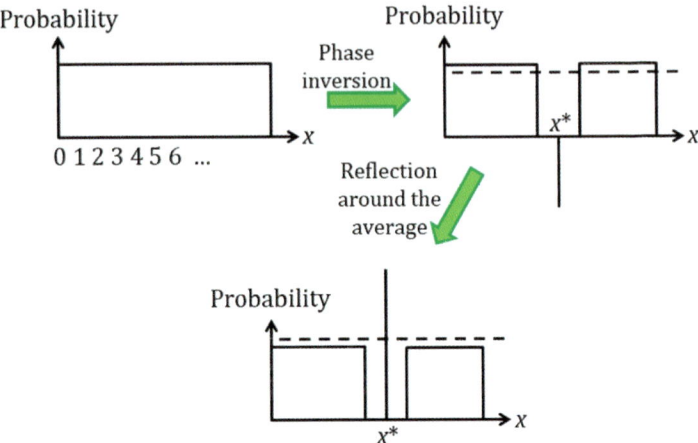

Figure 30. The observation probability for each piece of data in an unstructured database. A phase inversion only alters the 'needle', x^*, and the reflection around the average (represented by the dotted line) enhances the probability that the 'needle' will be observed.

---

[20] This probability will be reduced if Grover's algorithm is run too long.

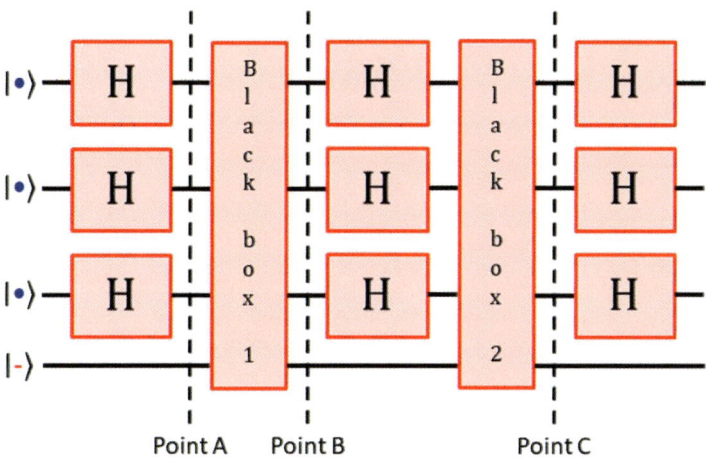

Figure 31. The quantum circuit for Grover's algorithm.

Summary of Chapter 5

- The role of a quantum computer is to manipulate the unseen data that is mostly destroyed after an observation

- There are five criteria for building a quantum computer

- Quantum decoherence, the interactions of qubits with their surroundings, is a major hurdle to overcome when constructing a quantum computer

- Recent advances in error correction techniques have helped overcome this difficulty

- If a quantum computer is not running a quantum algorithm, it is no different to an everyday computer

- For certain problems, quantum algorithms can produce solutions far more rapidly than regular algorithms

- On a viable quantum computer, Shor's algorithm could compromise encryption measures that are virtually unbreakable by regular algorithms

- Grover's algorithm can find a single piece of data within a 'sea of data' more quickly than any regular algorithms

6 NP-COMPLETE PROBLEMS: CAN QUANTUM COMPUTERS SOLVE THEM?

What are NP-Complete Problems?

In computer science, it is vital to determine the efficiency of an algorithm, i.e. how long a computational problem takes to be solved. In the previous chapter, we mentioned an algorithm that solves a certain problem in polynomial time. In simple terms this means that, when the difficulty of the problem is doubled, the solution takes four times longer to discover. The algorithm is less efficient when the solution is found at a slower speed than this; an example is the highly inefficient exponential time. The initials P and N in NP-complete stand for polynomial and non-deterministic, respectively. In this scenario, the latter relates to an 'amazing' computer that somehow guesses the answer instantly; this solution is then verified in polynomial time. An 'amazing' computer is completely theoretical, it is hoped that a quantum computer can someday serve in this role. If this is achievable, quantum algorithms would solve really difficult problems, i.e. those that are ordinarily unsolvable in polynomial time, at vastly quicker speeds. To summarise, NP-complete problems are solvable on a polynomial timescale using a hypothetical non-deterministic (potentially a quantum) method.[21]

---

[21] The 'complete' part of NP-complete means that we are dealing with the most difficult problems in NP. If an NP-complete problem is ever solved efficiently, all NP problems will be resolvable efficiently.

An example of an NP-complete problem is the travelling salesman problem (TSP).[22,23] TSP describes a salesman who travels between numerous cities, starting and finishing at the same place and visiting each destination only once. It can be modelled as an undirected weighted graph (Figure 32). The aim is to complete the task in minimal time using the smallest amount of resources. TSP is an optimisation problem in that the best solution is selected from all feasible solutions. The most obvious way to solve the TSP is with a brute-force method that, by trying every possible combination one-by-one, relies on sheer computing power rather than astute techniques to improve efficiency. Using a brute-force algorithm, if a 20-city problem is solved in 1 second, the TSP with 21, 22 and 30 cities has the solution in 21 seconds, 7 minutes and 3 million years, respectively. Fortunately, by breaking down the problem into smaller parts, special ways to improve the efficiency of the brute-force algorithm are possible. However, these algorithms are still remote from polynomial time: for example, 30 and 60 cities will take 10 minutes and 35,000 years, respectively.

The TSP is one of hundreds within the class known as 'hard' optimisation problems. Famously, at present, no solution in polynomial time is achievable for problems such as these. This fact has fascinated computer

---

[22] This problem was mathematically formulated by William Rowan Hamilton in the 1800s. His works on classical mechanics (which are mentioned in Chapter 2) are vital to the creation of quantum mechanics in the 20th century.

[23] Technically, and more precisely, the TSP is a NP-hard problem.

scientists and mathematicians for decades. Especially since an efficient solution to the travelling salesman problem, in particular, would lead to several applications in industry – including logistics, planning and the manufacture of microchips.

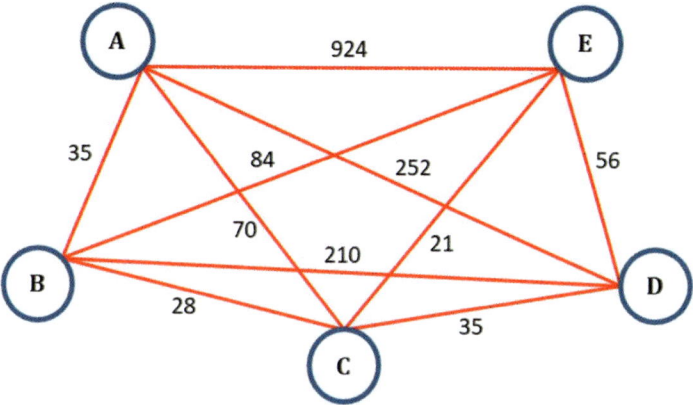

Figure 32. Undirected weighted graph for the travelling salesman problem with five cities (blue circles). Each city is connected to each other by the road, the air or the sea (red lines) and the numbers on each line are the weightings. The latter depends on the cost of travel, the time it takes to travel and the distance between cities.

Can Quantum Computers Solve NP-Complete Problems in Polynomial Time?

The short answer is we do not know.

Some researchers believe that quantum computers cannot solve NP-complete problems in polynomial time, but no definitive proof has been offered so far to support this position.

Shor's algorithm efficiently factorise integers, but factorising is not believed to be an NP-complete problem. In contrast, Grover's algorithm can be used to solve these types of problems but not in the polynomial time that is required. In fact, although the slower speed-up by this quantum algorithm is impressive, sophisticated regular algorithms can do better. Therefore, using Grover's algorithm to solve NP-complete problems is not a worthwhile enterprise.

Since the discovery of Shor's algorithm, a great deal of effort has been undertaken to find quantum algorithms that solve NP-complete problems in polynomial time. At the present time, we are still waiting for a possible solution.

Summary of Chapter 6

- NP-complete problems are a set of computational problems that are difficult to solve, but straightforward to verify

- NP-complete problems cannot be solved in polynomial time at present

- Quantum computing has been proposed as a tool to accomplish this goal

- It is debatable whether this is a future possibility or not

7 FUTURE OUTLOOK

In the last 20-30 years, the progress towards the creation of a quantum computer has been astounding. The mathematical groundwork for quantum computing is now well-established and new quantum algorithms are continually discovered all the time. In fact, the website Quantum Algorithm Zoo, which offers a comprehensive list of all known quantum algorithms, currently refers to 420 research papers on the subject. Unfortunately, however, the actual construction of a quantum computer is lagging behind. Qubit systems based on light, ions, anyons and superconductors have been proposed, but the large obstacle of quantum decoherence still has to be hurdled in all of them. Despite this, recent progress has been made on methods to circumvent this problem.

While it is true that all computational problems solved by a quantum computer can also be answered with an everyday computer, given enough resources and time. The revolutionary ability of a quantum computer is the extremely rapid speed that it solves certain difficult problems. This capability is attainable due to the harnessing of several quantum effects, including: (i) quantum superposition, which enables a vast amount of data to exist simultaneously in the input state; (ii) quantum interference, parts of the superposition can be either enhanced or suppressed, meaning that some outputs are more likely than others; (iii) non-determinism, different outcomes are possible for systems with the same input because nothing is for certain, only the probability of certain outcomes is known; (iv) quantum entanglement, correlations may exist between qubits so that an observation of one of them influences the others. All these effects are useful before an observation; after such an event, the system will act like a regular computer and the advantages are lost. The latter also occurs as a result of quantum decoherence.

Sometimes the media claim, mistakenly, that a huge amount of data can be processed simultaneously in a quantum computer, meaning that NP-complete problems can be solved instantly. There is some truth to the first part, but most of this data is lost after an observation – which is always required, otherwise no output will be obtainable. In addition, despite much progress, the press has overhyped the prospect of a large-scale quantum computer in the near future. But, in recent years, major advancements in quantum computing have been proclaimed by Big Tech. In 2019, Google declared 'quantum supremacy'; a milestone in which a quantum computer first outperformed any supercomputer. While, in the same year, IBM revealed that its innovative quantum computer contains 53 qubits, whereas Google announced the creation of a 72-qubit quantum chip the year before. In 2017, Microsoft introduced a programming language for quantum algorithms called Q sharp.

In 2011, D-Wave Systems believed they had constructed the first practical quantum computer. This was based on a technique known as quantum annealing, which is much easier to implement compared to a typical quantum computing model. However, the current scientific consensus is, for any interesting problem, that this method is unlikely to yield useful results. With the caveat that – due to the slight possibility of groundbreaking results – someone should be researching it. The manufacture of a large-scale quantum computer remains an extremely ambitious goal, possibly as remote as today's computers to people 60 years ago. Progress has undoubtedly been made, but it is difficult to predict, with much certainty, how rapidly quantum computing will develop in future.

APPENDIX

In a quantum computer, the rigid positioning of qubits in the quantum register is required. If the qubits are neutral particles (molecules) or electrically charged particles (ions) this positioning is achieved by using an optical or a static electric field lattice, respectively, which holds the particles in a two- or three-dimensional array (Figure A1).

An optical lattice is a set of nodes with a high light intensity; similar to the two-slit experiment, it is the interference pattern of laser beams that are travelling in opposite directions. Particles are attracted to the regions of high light intensity, due to the phenomenon known as optical trapping. As a result, a set of particles can reside at the nodes of the optical lattice and form an array. This can be visualised as analogous to eggs in a box: each particle (egg) is held in a rigid position by an energy minimum (a trough in the box). More information on optical lattices, and how light can influence neutral particles, can be found in a recent book by the author: D. L. Andrews and D. S. Bradshaw, Optical Nanomanipulation (Morgan & Claypool Publishers, San Rafael, CA, 2016).

When particles are electrically charged, trapping can be achieved by a quadrupole trap. Unlike neutral particles, the static electric fields produced by a quadrupole trap influence the positions of the charged particles.

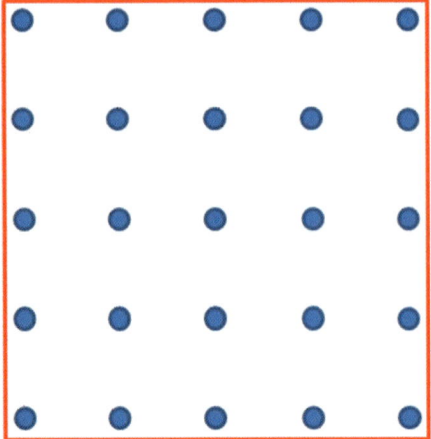

Fig. A1. Depiction of qubits (blue circles), in the form of atoms or ions, that are trapped in a set of rigid positions. In such a configuration, qubits in a quantum register can be labelled easily.

FURTHER READING

An Introduction to Quantum Computing by Phillip Kaye, Raymond Laflamme and Michele Mosca (Oxford University Press, Oxford, 2007)

Quantum Computing for Computer Scientists by Noson Yanofsky and Mirco Mannucci (Cambridge University Press, Cambridge, 2008)

Quantum Computing: A Short Course from Theory to Experiment by Joachim Stolze and Dieter Suter (Wiley-VCH, Weinheim, 2008)

Explorations in Quantum Computing by Colin Williams, 2nd Edition (Springer, London, 2011) – Highly Recommend

Quantum Computing: A Gentle Introduction by Eleanor Rieffel and Wolfgang Polak (MIT Press, Cambridge, MA, 2014) – Highly Recommend

Introduction to Photon Science and Technology by David Andrews and David Bradshaw (SPIE Press, Bellingham, WA, 2018)

Quantum Computing: An Applied Approach by Jack Hidary (Springer, Cham, Switzerland, 2019) – Highly Recommend

Quantum Computing for Everyone by Chris Bernhardt (MIT Press, Cambridge, MA, 2019)

GLOSSARY

Algorithm

A step-by-step process, or set of instructions, used by a computer to solve a problem.

AND gate

An irreversible logic gate for a regular computer. The output is 1 when both inputs are 1; otherwise it outputs a 0.

Atom

A tiny unit of matter, which consists of a nucleus circled by electrons.

Basis set

A set of elements used as a basis to describe any vector. The most common is the x, y and z axis (or Cartesian coordinates) used to define a vector in three-dimensional space. However, it is sometimes convenient to express a vector with a different base set. For example, a spherical coordinate system that involves angles between the x, y and z axis and the vector. In short, a vector can be described with various basis sets.

Bell state

Named after John Bell, it is the simplest quantum state for entangled qubits.

Bell tests

A set of experiments designed to test the theory of quantum mechanics. To date, they all agree with Bell's theorem.

Bell's theorem

Introduced by John Bell in 1964, the theorem mathematically proves that the local hidden variables of the EPR paradox are inconsistent with reality.

Bit

A unit of data in everyday computing. It has one of two values, either 0 or 1.

Bit flip

A quantum logic gate that interchanges the qubit state $|\bullet\rangle$ into $|\bullet\rangle$ or *vice-versa*

Black box

In computing, a black box is an object that has inputs and

outputs but the internal processes are unknown.

Bloch sphere

Named after Felix Bloch, the positions on its surface graphically represent the quantum states of a qubit.

Bra-ket notation

First used by Paul Dirac, it represents a quantum state.

Byte

A set of eight bits.

Capacitor

A device used to store electrical charge, consisting of a pair of electrodes separated by an insulator.

Charge

When particles have electrical charge it means that, when they are placed into an electric field, a force is applied to them. A typical example is the flow of negatively-charged electrons within an electronic circuit.

Classical physics

The physics of everyday, macroscopic objects. It is also

known as Newtonian physics.

Collapse of the wavefunction

An irreversible event that occurs when a quantum system is observed. Only one of the two quantum states of a single qubit exists afterwards.

Complex number

A useful mathematical device used in numerous scientific fields. A complex number is expressible as $c + id$, where c and d are real numbers and i is the imaginary unit; the square of such a unit equals -1. The imaginary unit arises because the square root of a negative number cannot be represented by a real number. The complex conjugate of such a number simply involves a change in sign on the imaginary term, i.e. $c - id$. A complex number multiplied by its complex conjugate produces a real number (the terms with imaginary units cancel out).

Compton scattering

Discovered by Arthur Compton, it is the scattering of a photon by an electron.

Controlled-NOT gate

A quantum logic gate that, when the control qubit is in state $|●\rangle$, interchanges the target qubit from $|●\rangle$ to $|●\rangle$ or *vice-versa*.

Cooper pairs

A pair of electrons bound together at low temperatures, first described by Leon Cooper. The Cooper pair is responsible for superconductivity.

Cryptography

A method of protecting information via codes, so that only intended people can access it.

Current

The flow of electrons in an electronic circuit.

Deterministic model

A system that always produces the same outcome from known initial conditions. There is no randomness to the future of such a system.

DiVincenzo's five criteria

First proposed by David DiVincenzo, they are the five conditions for construction of a quantum computer.

Double-slit experiment

First performed by Thomas Young in 1801, it demonstrates that light can display both wave and particle characteristics.

Electrode

A conductor through which electricity enters or leaves an object.

Electrons

Negatively-charged particles that are found in atoms.

EPR paradox

The Einstein-Podolsky-Rosen paradox is a thought experiment that argues that the description of quantum mechanics is incomplete. It was proved wrong by John Bell.

Exponential time

An inefficient speed for an algorithm. It is much slower than polynomial time.

Factorisation (factoring)

A decomposition of a number or mathematical expression into a simpler form, for example 4 and 8 are factors of 32 or $x^2 + 8x + 16 = (x + 4)(x + 4)$.

Grover's algorithm

A quantum algorithm for searching unstructured databases, discovered by Lov Grover in 1996.

Hadamard gate

A quantum logic gate that converts qubit states in the standard basis to the sign basis or *vice-versa*. It can split a single quantum state into two states in a superposition.

Hard disk drives

A long-term data storage device for regular computing.

Heisenberg's microscope

A thought experiment, by Werner Heisenberg, that provides an explanation for his uncertainty principle.

Inductor

A coil of wire, often twisted around a steel or iron core, which acts as an electromagnet.

Insulator

Material that does not conduct electricity.

Interferometer

An instrument in which the interference of two light beams is used to make precise measurements.

Ions

Atoms containing an electrical charge.

Josephson junction

A Josephson junction is a thin layer of non-super-conducting material sandwiched between two layers of superconducting material. It is named after Brian Josephson, who predicted in 1962 that pairs of electrons can quantum tunnel through the non-superconducting barrier in such a junction.

Laser beam

A device, first built in 1960, which emits light that is highly coherent. Laser is an acronym for light amplification by stimulated emission of radiation.

Logic gate

Electronic device that is the basic building block of any digital system. Examples include AND, OR and NOT gates.

Magnetic domains

A region of a magnetic material in which the magnetization is in a uniform direction.

Measurements

The irreversible act of observing a quantum system.

Molecules

A set of electrically-neutral atoms that are held together by chemical bonds.

Newton's Laws

Three physical laws that lay the foundation for classical physics.

No-cloning principle

The theorem that says it is impossible to create an identical copy of an unknown quantum state.

Normalisation condition

In quantum theory, the probabilities of all the states in a system always add up to 1.

NOT gate

A reversible logic gate for a regular computer. The output is 1 when the input is 0 or *vice-versa*.

NP-complete problems

Any set of computational problems for which no efficient algorithm has been found.

Phase flip

A quantum logic gate that interchanges the phase of a qubit, so that $|+\rangle$ becomes $|-\rangle$ or *vice-versa*.

Photoelectric effect

The emission of electrons from a metal surface when light is shone onto the metal.

Physical property

A characteristic of an object that is measurable.

Polarised light

In a polarised transverse wave, such as light, the oscillations travel in a certain linear or circular direction perpendicular to the propagation direction.

Polynomial time

An efficient speed for an algorithm. It is much faster than exponential time.

Potential energy

Energy possessed by an object that is not kinetic. For example, an object positioned at a height has gravitational potential energy.

Probability distribution

A set of values that give the probability of a certain possibility actually occurring. For example, the probability distribution of a fair coin toss is 0.5 for heads and 0.5 for tails. The probability that heads or tails will occur is 1 (0.5 + 0.5), i.e. no other outcome is possible. When the coin is flipped and a head (or a tail) is observed, the probability of that outcome becomes one (i.e. the result is then known with certainty).

Projectiles

Any object that is thrown, fired or flung by a force.

Quantum algorithms

Algorithms that use quantum phenomena. They solve certain computational problems much more quickly than regular algorithms.

Quantum circuit

A quantum computational model that involves a sequence of quantum gates with wires carrying qubits to and from them.

Quantum coin

A representation of a qubit. It works on the principle that two outcomes are possible for both a coin and a qubit.

Quantum computer

A computer based on quantum mechanics.

Quantum decoherence

A loss of quantum behaviour due to the interaction of the qubit with its surroundings or environment.

Quantum entanglement

The connection between a pair, or group, of quantum systems.

Quantum interference

Interference within a quantum system. It produces the fringe patterns in the two-slit experiment.

Quantum logic gates

The building blocks of quantum circuits that modifies the state of the qubits.

Quantum mechanics

The theory that describes the physical properties of particles at the nanoscale.

Quantum register

A system in a quantum computer that contains multiple qubits.

Quantum superposition

Two or more quantum states that exist, simultaneously, before an observation.

Quantum teleportation

The process of transferring quantum information from one location to another.

Quantum tunnelling

The quantum mechanical ability of a particle to tunnel through a potential energy barrier.

Qubit

The unit of data in a quantum computer.

Qubyte

A set of eight qubits.

Random access memory

A short-term data storage device for regular computing.

Resistance

An electrical quantity that is a measure of the reduction of current in a circuit.

Reversible gates

A logic gate in a computer that, in principle, does not dissipate heat. They are essential in quantum computing.

Schrödinger's Cat

A thought experiment devised by Erwin Schrödinger. It is the scenario in which a hypothetical cat is simultaneously alive and dead, in a quantum superposition.

Speed up

In computer science, it is a measure of the relative performance of two algorithms processing the same problem.

Shor's algorithm

Discovered by Peter Shor in 1994, it is the first quantum algorithm for factorisation.

Special relativity

Albert Einstein's postulate that the speed of light in a vacuum is the same for all observers.

Squeezed light

A quantum state of electromagnetic radiation.

Superconductor

The ability of an electrical conductor to have zero resistance at very low temperatures.

Toffoli gate

A reversible logic gate identical to a controlled-NOT gate, except a second control bit (or qubit) is included.

Topological quantum computing

A theoretical quantum computer based on anyons.

Transistors

A device used to either amplify electronic signals or act

as a switch.

Uncertainty Principle

Proposed by Heisenberg in 1927, it is the quantum mechanical principle that position and momentum of a particle cannot be known simultaneously.

Voltage

The difference in electric potential between two points.

Wave-Particle Duality

The quantum mechanical concept that light (or an electron) acts like a particle and a wave.

Wavefunction

A description of the potentialities that may become realities in a quantum system.

BIOGRAPHICAL

Profiles on the classical and quantum physicists mentioned in Chapter 2.

Classical era

Aristotle (384-322 B.C.E.)

Aristotle was a philosopher from Ancient Greece.

Born in 384 B.C.E. in the North Eastern Greek city of Stagira, Aristotle was sent to Athens at the age of seventeen to study in Plato's Academy. After Plato's death in 347 B.C.E. he left for Assos, in Asia Minor, on the northwest coast of present-day Turkey and next moved to the coastal island of Lesbos three years later. In both of these locations, he continued the philosophical activity that he began at the Academy. While in Lesbos, Aristotle married Pythias with whom he had a daughter.

In 343 B.C.E., at the request of the King Philip II of Macedon, Aristotle left Lesbos for Pella (the Macedonian capital) to tutor the king's thirteen-year-old son – who later became Alexander the Great. Remaining in Macedon after completion of his tutoring commitments, it was not until 343 B.C.E. that he returned to Athens. Here Aristotle set up his own school, called the Lyceum, dedicated to the god Apollo Lykeios. The Lyceum conducted research into a wide range of subjects: botany, biology, logic, music, mathematics, astronomy, medicine, cosmology, physics, philosophy, metaphysics, psychology, ethics, theology, rhetoric, political theory, rhetoric and the arts. By collecting manuscripts in all these areas, his school was able to assemble the first great library of antiquity. During this time, Aristotle's wife died and he started a relationship with Herpyllis. They had children together and she was probably his wife at the time of his death.

In 323 B.C.E. he again left Athens, where anti-Macedonian sentiments were rapidly amplifying. Because of his connections to Macedon he fled to Chalcis, on the island of Euboea. He stated: "I will not allow the Athenians to sin twice against philosophy" – a reference to the trial and execution of Socrates in Athens in 399 B.C.E. Aristotle died on Euboea of natural causes in 322 B.C.E.

Francis Bacon (1561-1626)

Francis Bacon was an English philosopher and statesman.

Born in London in 1561, he was the second child of Nicholas Bacon and his second wife Lady Anne Bacon. Alongside his elder brother, between 1573 and 1575, he went to Trinity College in Cambridge. Their tutor was John Whitgift, the Archbishop of Canterbury in later life. From 1577 to 1578 he accompanied Sir Amias Paulet, the

English Ambassador to Paris, on a diplomatic mission. When his father died in 1579, he returned to England and campaigned for a seat in the House of Commons. In 1581, he was elected Member of Parliament for Bossiney in Cornwall; the first of his thirty-seven years in office. Following his studies at Gray's Inn, he was admitted to the bar in 1582. Fifteen years later, Francis Bacon became the first person to be designated the Queen's Counsel; the legal representative of the Crown.

From an early age, Bacon aimed to revise natural philosophy and to formulate an outline for a new system of the sciences. His intentions received very little support from others, especially Queen Elizabeth who wanted him to work on more pressing matters. It was clear that it would be difficult for him to overcome the intellectual backwardness, and dogmatic blockades, of his age. The year before his manufactured impeachment for corruption in 1621, he published the book "Novum Organum" (New organon, or true directions concerning the interpretation of nature). This work details a new system of logic, centred on experimental research, which became known as the Baconian method; it is instrumental in the historical development of the scientific method, acting as the inspiration for the formation of the Royal Society in 1660.

Having lost all of his prestigious positions, Bacon devoted the last five years of his life – known as the quinquennium – exclusively to natural philosophy. This was a huge undertaking that, despite his great efforts, was too much to fully accomplish in a few years. Following an experiment using snow as a preserver of meat, he died in London of pneumonia in 1626. Unfortunately, the proverb – often quoted in his works – proved to be true: "Vita brevis, ars longa" (Art is long, life is short).

Galileo Galilei (1564-1642)

Galileo Galilei was an Italian astronomer, physicist and philosopher.

The son of a musician, Galileo Galilei was born in 1564 near the Italian city of Pisa. He started to study medicine at the University of Pisa, but soon changed his subjects to philosophy and mathematics. Numerous years later, in 1589, he became professor of mathematics at Pisa. There he demonstrated – by dropping items of differing weights from the top of the Leaning Tower of Pisa – that the free-fall speed of an object is not proportional to its weight, which was the claim of Aristotle. He wrote the manuscript "De motu" (On Motion), which abandoned Aristotelian ideas about motion. Due to his perceived attack on Aristotle, Galileo became unpopular with his colleagues and his contract was not renewed. He moved to the University of Padua in 1592.

After the death of his father in 1591, his responsibilities as the head of the family meant that he was always chronically short of money. His university salary did not cover all his expenses, so he tutored privately to make-up for any shortfall. He never married, perhaps due to his financial problems, but Galileo did have two daughters and a son with a Venetian woman called Marina Gamba. Continuing his research, Galileo determined in 1609 that the trajectory of a projectile is a parabola, which again contradicts Aristotelian physics. In the same year, he heard about the invention of the telescope in the Netherlands and constructed his own superior version without having seen it. He was awarded with a life tenure, a doubling of salary and he became famous. With his new apparatus, his discoveries included mountains and valleys on the moon, sunspots and the four largest moons of Jupiter. In 1610, he returned to his home region as court mathematician and philosopher in Florence.

Galileo's discoveries reinforced his belief that the Sun is the centre of the universe and Earth is just a planet revolving around it. This aligned with the 67 year-old ideas (at that time) of Nicolaus Copernicus. In 1614, Galileo was accused of heresy by the church for his support of the Copernican theory; he was banned from discussing his ideas on the subject in public. He was condemned a second time, in 1632, following publication of "Dialogo sopra i due massimi sistemi del mondo, tolemaico e copernicano" (Dialogue Concerning the Two Chief World Systems - Ptolemaic and Copernican). In this book, he provided arguments for and against the Copernican theory via a discussion between three men. One of which was often ridiculed, but his viewpoint at the end of the book represented the one favoured by Pope Urban VIII (who reigned between 1623 and 1644). Galileo was summoned before the Inquisition in Rome in 1633. There he was convicted and sentenced to life imprisonment, later reduced to house arrest at a villa near Florence. He was forced to publicly denounce Copernican theory.

Despite his failing eyesight, Galileo finished writing his unpublished studies, which had been interrupted by his interest in telescopes, for his final manuscript "Discorsi e dimostrazioni matematiche intorno a due nuove scienze attenenti alla meccanica" (Dialogues Concerning Two New Sciences). This was published in 1638; it provided an account of his ideas on the laws of motion and the principles of mechanics. Four years later he died at the villa that had been his prison for eight years.

Isaac Newton (1642-1727)

Isaac Newton was an English mathematician, physicist and astronomer.

In the year that Galileo died and the English Civil War began, Newton was born in Woolsthorpe (near Grantham) to a Puritan family. After leaving boarding school in Grantham, he studied at Trinity College, Cambridge, from 1661. Here he was educated in Aristotelian rhetoric, logic, ethics and physics. By 1664, he was also teaching himself mathematics. From 1665-1667, he returned home because of the plague. His *annus mirabilis* (miraculous year) was during this time, in which he made revolutionary discoveries in mathematics, motion, optics and gravitation. It was in this period that, after observing an apple falling from a tree, he hit upon the theory of gravity. He also became the world-wide leading mathematician, following his creation of calculus. In 1667, he returned to Trinity as a Fellow and then became Lucasian Professor of Mathematics in 1669. He continued in this role for the next thirty-three years. During these years, alongside his many scientific studies, Isaac Newton began his more private research into alchemy and theology.

By the late 1670s, Newton had become more and more secluded, mainly because of his disillusionment with the criticism of his work by leading scientists of the time. This isolation forcibly changed in 1687 with the publication of the "Principia" (Mathematical Principles of Natural Philosophy). This book propelled Newton towards his designation as one of the great scientists of natural philosophy. Yet, despite widespread acclaim in England, his work was less influential on the European continent because prominent scientists there, such as Huygens and Leibniz, still opposed his theory of gravity. It was not until after Newton's death, when his ideas were progressively verified in mainline Europe, that Newton became equally admired there. In fact, what is now regarded as 'Newtonian Mechanics' or 'Newtonian Physics' mostly derive from these findings in continental

Europe between 1740 and 1800.

In the years that followed the publication of his famous manuscript, Newton showed interest in obtaining positions of power in London. He accomplished some minor roles, attained because of the reverence for his scientific achievements rather than any ability as a statesman. Newton moved to London to become the Warden of the Royal Mint in 1696 and then the Master of the Mint for 28 years from 1699. Both appointments were considered sinecures, but he took them very seriously. Newton was twice Member of Parliament for Cambridge University in 1689 and 1701, but his only contribution was to request that a window be closed to stop a draught in the chamber. He was President of the Royal Society from 1703 until his death in 1727. After his passing, Newton's hair was found to contain large quantities of mercury that pertained to his alchemical pursuits; the resultant mercury poisoning probably explains his eccentric behaviour in later life.

Joseph-Louis Lagrange (1736-1813)

Joseph-Louis Lagrange was an Italian mathematician, physicist and astronomer; he was later a naturalised citizen of France.

He was born Giuseppe Lodovico Lagrangia in Turin, Italy, in 1736. Lagrange had both Italian and French descent; his paternal great-grandfather was a French army officer who had moved to Turin. His father was Treasurer of the Office of Public Works and Fortifications for Turin, but later lost most of his wealth due to failed investments. Lagrange would later say: "If I had been rich, I probably would not have devoted myself to mathematics". Lagrange was originally primed for a career as a lawyer: his favourite subject at the University of Turin was Latin and he had very little enthusiasm for mathematics, especially geometry. However, all that changed when he inadvertently read a paper by the astronomer Edmond Halley, which lead to a lifelong and self-taught devotion to mathematics.

At only 19 years old, Lagrange was appointed Assistant Professor of Mathematics at the Royal Military Academy of the Theory and Practice of Artillery in Turin. There he taught courses on calculus and mechanics in support of the Piedmontese army's early adoption of ballistics theory. In the same year, Lagrange began his correspondence with the renowned Swiss Mathematician Leonhard Euler. Recognising his exceptional talent, Euler aided the attempts to entice Lagrange to a prestigious position in Prussia. Not seeking greatness, and only wanting to devote all his time to mathematics, he politely refused the position. He would finally relent, after a number of years, and accepted a post in Berlin in 1766; he would work there for the next 20 years. A year later he married his cousin Vittoria Conti, but they never had any children.

Turin, and the Italian states, had always regretted

losing Lagrange to Prussia. They constantly tried to lure him back to Italy, but he considered Berlin the ideal place for producing his mathematics undisturbed. However, when his wife died in 1783 and then his friend Frederick II of Prussia in 1786, Berlin was less appealing to him. Despite the Italian states best efforts, the opportunity to move to Paris (along with the promise that there were no teaching commitments) was too great. Lagrange moved to Paris in 1787; he would later survive the French Revolution and remained in Paris for the rest of his career. His survival of the Reign of Terror is attributed to his quote: "I believe that, in general, one of the first principles of every wise man is to conform strictly to the laws of the country in which he is living, even when they are unreasonable". He died in Paris in 1813.

Thomas Young (1773-1829)

Thomas Young was an English polymath, especially known as a mathematician and physicist.

Born in 1773, he was the eldest of ten children in a Quaker family from Milverton, Somerset. In 1792, he went to study medicine at St Bartholomew's Hospital in London and then moved to the University of Edinburgh Medical School in 1794. As a Quaker he could not study at Oxford or Cambridge, so he could only obtain a degree from a Scottish university at that time in Britain. Two years later he attained a doctorate in medicine from the University of Göttingen, Germany. A rule change had meant, to qualifying to practice medicine, he was required to study at the same university for two years. By leaving the Quakers, and declaring himself Church of England, he was able to enter Emmanuel College, Cambridge, in 1797. Although enrolled to study medicine, Young already had more than sufficient knowledge on the subject; so he spent most of his time learning physics and mathematics by himself. In the same year, he became financially secure when he inherited the estate of his great-uncle. In 1799, he established himself as a physician in London.

In 1801, he accepted an approach to lecture at the Royal Institution in London; he resigned in 1803, to concentrate on his medical practice. In 1804, Young married Eliza Maxwell but they never had children. In the same year, he was made foreign secretary to the Royal Society for life. Expanding on his lectures at the Royal Institution, in 1807 Young published a two-volume work that provided more evidence to support the wave theory of light. This contradicted Newton's ideas, so it was inevitably ridiculed by most scientists at that time. The manuscript also contained a mechanics lecture on elasticity, in which Young's modulus is first introduced. He continued to try to build his medical practice but, despite being a talented physician, his bedside manner was lacking. His practice was not having great successes because of this. Young was appointed to the St. George's Hospital in 1811, but failed to make any impression there in spite of his diligent efforts. His achievements outside of medicine probably hindered his career within the field. Starting in 1814, in yet another field that interested him, Young endeavoured to decipher the Rosetta stone. In the end, all the plaudits went to the French linguist Champollion, who failed to acknowledge Young's major contributions to the task.

In 1816, the French scientist François Arago visited Young to discuss Fresnel's experiments on the wave theory of light. Young would later visit Arago in Paris in 1817 and 1821. Despite having outstanding health for most of his life, it began to deteriorate in 1828 while on a visit to Geneva. His continuous breathing problems eventually led to his death in 1829 in London. Perhaps due to the difficulties he had in communicating his ideas, his immense and wide-ranging achievements received little recognition in his day. Sadly, this opinion was clearly made by Arago in his eulogy to him: "The death of Young in his own country attracted but little regard".

Augustin-Jean Fresnel (1788-1827)

Augustin-Jean Fresnel was a French civil engineer and physicist.

Born in Broglie in Normandy in 1788, his father was an architect and he was one of four siblings. As a child he showed no real signs of brilliance. However, following a substantial upturn in his academic performance, Fresnel was accepted into the École Polytechnique in Paris in 1804. After graduating in 1806, he joined École des

Ponts et Chaussées and qualified as a civil engineer a few years later. He was employed by Corps des Ponts et Chaussées; he would work there for the rest of his career. It was in 1812, when Fresnel was sent to assist the construction of the imperial highway between Spain and Italy, that evidence of his interest in optics first emerged.

In 1815, after remarking that Napoleon's return to France from Elba was "an attack on civilization", he offered his services to the royalist resistance but his sickly nature made him a wretched soldier. By departing from work without leave, and returning to death threats from colleagues, he was placed on suspension for all of the Hundred Days War. During this period, he worked on the optics experiments that convinced him that the wave theory of light was accurate; although, at that time, this idea was totally rejected in favour of Newton's corpuscular (particle) theory. Unaware of the findings on this subject by Thomas Young circa 1798, Fresnel produced a similar investigation that, crucially, developed a mathematical formulation for the wave theory. Following the defeat of Napoleon at Waterloo, he was reinstated as a civil engineer and, as a result, had much less time for his research. The latter included the work, with François Arago, on a novel lens for lighthouses. It was first installed in 1823 and became known as "the invention that saved a million ships". The Fresnel lantern, which also uses this lens, is commonly used in the theatre.

Due to constant bad health, he retired at the age of

thirty-six and ceased his scientific research. Soon after this retirement, in 1824, he would say: "I could have wished to live longer, because I perceive that there are in the inexhaustible range of science, a great number of questions of public utility, of which, perhaps, I might have had the happiness of finding the solution". The Royal Society presented him with the Rumford Medal, an award for outstanding research in the field of the physics, while he was on his death bed. He died from tuberculosis on Bastille Day in 1827.

William Rowan Hamilton (1805-1865)

William Rowan Hamilton was an Irish mathematician, astronomer and physicist.

Born in Dublin in 1805, he was the fourth of nine children. Immensely talented from an early age, he had learned many modern European Languages, Latin, Persian, Arabic, Hindustani, Sanskrit, Marathi, Malay and Hebrew by the age of thirteen. His interest in mathematics arose following his defeat to the American child prodigy, Zerah Colburn, in mental arithmetic – who was exhibited in Dublin in 1813. At the age of eighteen, he entered Trinity College in Dublin to study both the classics and mathematics. He would receive an optime in both subjects, an off-the-charts distinction that was very rarely awarded; it was a feat that was truly unique. He also won awards for his poetry, which would lead to a life-long friendship with the famous poet William

Wordsworth. While still an undergraduate, in 1827, he was selected Andrews Professor of Astronomy. In 1833, he married Helen Bayly; despite a difficult marriage, they had three children together.

After his discovery, in the same year, that complex numbers can be expressed as algebraic couples, he obsessively tried to extend it to triplets over many years. Even his children were well aware of this preoccupation, every morning they asked: "Well, Papa can you multiply triplets?". This fixation, along with problems in his personal life, would lead to depression and heavy drinking. In 1843, while walking along the Royal Canal with his wife, in a flash of genius he created quaternions; the formulae for which he carved into a nearby stone bridge. Despite misgivings by fellow scientists, he believed that his discovery would revolutionise mathematical physics; Hamilton would spend the rest of his life exploring them. He published "Lectures on Quaternions" in 1853, but he soon realised that his work was poorly presented in it, perhaps exposing Hamilton's lack of skills as a teacher. In an attempt to produce a long-lasting book of quality, Hamilton began to write "Elements of Quaternions" in 1859. With the final chapter of his 800-page book incomplete, he died following a severe attack of gout in 1865.

Quantum era

Albert Einstein (1879-1955)

Albert Einstein was a German theoretical physicist.

He was born in Ulm, Germany, in 1879. His father, who was an engineer and a salesman, moved the family to Munich six weeks later. They then relocated to Italy a number of years later. Einstein joined the Swiss Federal Polytechnic School in Zurich in 1896, where he trained as a physics and mathematics teacher. He met Mileva Marić while studying there and they married in 1903. In 1901, after attaining his diploma and acquiring Swiss citizenship, he accepted a position as technical assistant at the Swiss Patent Office. While working as a patent agent in 1905, Einstein had his *annus mirabilis* (miraculous year); he wrote four research papers, in his spare time, that substantially contributed to the foundation of modern physics.

By 1908, now recognized as a prominent scientist, he was appointed Lecturer at the University of Bern and then, in 1909, Associate Professor at the University of Zürich. He would become full Professor at the University of Prague in 1911; by accepting this role, he also became an Austrian citizenship in the Austro-Hungarian Empire. A year later, he returned to Zürich as a full Professor. In 1914, we joined the University of Berlin; a decision influenced by the prospect of living near his cousin Elsa, who became his second wife in 1919. During the 1920s, he lectured in Europe, America and the Far East. He was awarded the 1921 Nobel Prize in Physics "for his services to Theoretical Physics and especially for his discovery of the law of the photoelectric effect". Einstein would remain at the University of Berlin until the early 1930s.

He became a German citizen in 1914 but renounced it in 1933, because of the rise of Hitler. He accepted a post at the Institute for Advanced Study in Princeton, New Jersey, and became an American citizen in 1940. Einstein died in Princeton in 1955 from internal bleeding due to an abdominal aortic aneurysm. He had requested that his body be cremated, but the Princeton pathologist Thomas Harvey removed his brain during his autopsy, without permission, in order to discover the secrets of his genius. The remains of Einstein's brain reside at the National Museum of Health and Medicine near Washington D.C.

Erwin Schrödinger (1887-1961)

Erwin Schrödinger was an Austrian physicist.

Born in 1887 in Vienna, he was the only child of Rudolf Schrödinger and the daughter of Alexander Bauer, Professor of Chemistry at the Technical College of Vienna. He was highly gifted from an early age, his broad range of interests included philosophy, logic, physics, poetry and psychology. From 1906, he studied physics at the University of Vienna. During the Great War, he served as an artillery officer. He then held positions at Jena, Stuttgart, Breslau and Zurich from 1920 to 1926. Schrödinger struggled with tuberculosis; in the 1920s, he stayed several times at a sanatorium in Switzerland. It was there that he discovered his famous wave equation. In 1927, he succeeded Max Planck at the Friedrich Wilhelm University in Berlin. At that time, the German capital was the centre of great scientific activity. In 1933, due to his dislike of Nazi ideology, he left Germany to become a Fellow of Magdalen College at the University of Oxford. In the same year, he was jointly awarded the Nobel Prize in Physics with Paul Dirac "for the discovery of new productive forms of atomic theory".

His position at Oxford soon became untenable, primarily because of the disapproval he received over his domestic arrangements. Schrödinger married Anne-Marie Bertel in 1920, but also lived with his mistress Hilde March; who was the wife of an Austrian colleague and mother of Schrödinger's one-year-old daughter. This unconventional arrangement would create tenure issues for him in the years that followed. In this period, following extensive correspondence with Albert Einstein, he proposed what is now called the Schrödinger's cat thought experiment. In 1938, he received a personal invitation from the Taoiseach to reside in Ireland and help develop the Institute for Advanced Studies in Dublin. He accepted, took Irish citizenship and remained there until his retirement in 1955. During his time in Dublin, he wrote a book in 1944 that provided speculation on how genetic information could be stored in molecules. This work inspired Crick and Watson to discover the double helix structure of DNA in 1953. Schrödinger died of tuberculosis in Vienna in 1961.

Werner Heisenberg (1901-1976)

Werner Heisenberg was a German physicist.

He was born in 1901 in Würzburg, Germany, to Annie Wecklein and Dr. August Heisenberg, who later became Professor of the Medieval and Modern Greek languages. From 1920 to 1923, he studied physics and mathematics at the University of Munich and the University of Göttingen. In 1926, he was appointed Lecturer in Theoretical Physics at the University of Copenhagen and, a year later, he accepted the position of Professor of Theoretical Physics at the University of Leipzig. In 1929, he went on a lecture tour to the United States, Japan and India. In the same year, alongside Wolfgang Pauli, he wrote a paper that laid the foundation for relativistic quantum field theory. Heisenberg was awarded the Nobel Prize for Physics in 1932 "for the creation of quantum mechanics, the application of which has, inter alia, led to the discovery of the allotropic forms of hydrogen". In 1937, he married Elisabeth Schumacher and they had seven children.

Unlike other scientists at that time, Heisenberg refused any invitation to immigrate to the United States after Hitler came to power. Yet, the Nazis would constantly block his appointment to prominent roles in Germany. The matter was somewhat resolved when Heisenberg's mother visited Heinrich Himmler's mother (a family acquaintance) and Himmler was persuaded to intervene on his behalf. Eventually, in 1942, Heisenberg was appointed Director of the Kaiser Wilhelm Institute for Physics at the University of Berlin. At the end of World War 2 he, and other German physicists, were detained by American troops and imprisoned in England. In 1946, after his return to Germany, he helped reorganise the Institute for Physics at Göttingen; in 1948, it was renamed the Max Planck Institute for Physics. Still Director of the Institute in 1955, he moved to Munich when it was relocated there. He was also appointed, in 1958, Professor of Physics at the University of Munich. Heisenberg retired from his institute directorship in 1970; he died of kidney cancer in Munich in 1976.

Paul Dirac (1902-1984)

Paul Dirac was an English physicist.

He was born in 1902 in Bristol, England, to a Swiss father and English mother. Dirac was one of three children. His father insisted that his children be Swiss citizens, but this changed in 1919 when his father attained British citizenship. He had an unhappy childhood, mainly because his parents despised each other. His father spoke only French and his mother only

English so that, in his earliest years, he believed that men and women spoke different languages. His father was a strict authoritarian that forced him to speak French; he would hardly speak at all to avoid making inevitable mistakes. His silent nature would continue for the rest of his life.

He studied electrical engineering and mathematics at Bristol University from 1918. It soon became clear that his mathematical abilities were extraordinary, but his skills in the laboratory were mediocre at best. He then moved to St. John's College, Cambridge, as a research student in mathematics. After graduating in 1927, he became a Fellow at the College and, in 1932, Lucasian Professor of Mathematics at Cambridge. In 1928, he predicted the existence of an electron with a positive (rather than a negative) charge; this was discovered four years later. Another of his great achievements, at that time, was the formulation of quantum electrodynamics – a description of the interaction of light and matter using quantum theory. Dirac would travel extensively in the 1920s and 1930s and worked at various foreign universities. In 1933, he was jointly awarded the Nobel Prize in Physics with Erwin Schrödinger "for the discovery of new productive forms of atomic theory". In 1937, he married Margit Wigner from Budapest, Hungary, who was the sister of a prominent theoretical physicist. In 1969, he retired from his Chair at Cambridge and moved to Tallahassee, Florida. He later accepted a position at Florida State University. Dirac died in Tallahassee in 1984. A commemorative marker, created in his honour, was unveiled at Westminster Abbey in 1995.

David Bohm (1917-1992)

David Bohm was an American physicist.

He was born in Wilkes-Barre, Pennsylvania, to an immigrant Jewish family in 1917. Bohm attended Pennsylvania State University, he graduated in 1939, and then the California Institute of Technology. Afterwards, he worked under Robert Oppenheimer at the University of California, Berkeley. In his youth, he was involved in radical politics; he was active in communist organizations, such as the Young Communist League. After the war, Bohm became an Assistant Professor at Princeton University. But his political activism as a younger man caught up with him, when he was called before the House Un-American Activities Committee in 1949. Bohm declared his Fifth Amendment right to refuse to testify; although he was eventually acquitted, Princeton had already suspended him and refused to reinstate him. Bohm left the United States for Brazil, so that he could undertake a Professorship at the University of São Paulo in 1951. He moved to England from 1957, first working at the University of Bristol and then, between 1961 until his retirement in 1987, at the University of London. In 1992, Bohm died after suffering a heart attack in London.

Richard Feynman (1918-1988)

Richard Feynman was an American physicist.

Born in 1918 in New York City, his father was originally from Minsk in Belarus. He did not speak until after his third birthday. Later, still as a child, he had a real talent for engineering; he especially enjoyed repairing radios. Studying mathematics, electrical engineering and then physics, he graduated from Massachusetts Institute of Technology in 1939. He then moved to Princeton and received his Doctorate in 1942. After the war, in 1945, Feynman was appointed Professor of Theoretical Physics at Cornell University. In 1950, he accepted the same role at the California Institute of Technology; where he remained for the rest of his career. Feynman was co-awarded the 1965 Nobel Prize in Physics, jointly with Sin-Itiro Tomonaga and Julian Schwinger, "for fundamental work in quantum electrodynamics, with deep-ploughing consequences for the physics of elementary particles".

In early 1979, his health began to deteriorate. After his recovery from surgery, he became a famous public figure following the surprising big success of his books. His last major task was as a member of a committee that investigated the explosion on the space shuttle Challenger in 1986. His abdominal cancer re-appeared during this time and he died in 1988 in Los Angeles. His final words where: "I'd hate to die twice. It's so boring". A day after his death, the Soviet government finally authorised his visit to the Tuvan Autonomous Soviet Socialist Republic; a life-time ambition of Feynman. His daughter would later make the journey in his place.

John Bell (1928-1990)

John Bell was a physicist from Northern Ireland.

Born in Belfast in 1928, his ancestors had lived in the north of Ireland for many generations. From 1945, Bell studied physics at Queen's University, Belfast, and later at the University of Birmingham in England. In 1949, he began his career at the Atomic Energy Research Establishment in Oxfordshire, but soon moved to the accelerator physics group at Malvern, Worcestershire. He met Mary Ross there and they had a successful marriage from 1954 onwards. Numerous years later, he went to work for the European Organization for Nuclear Research (CERN), in Geneva, Switzerland. He spent the rest of his career there. During a year's leave from CERN, in 1964, he spent his time at Stanford University, the University of Wisconsin-Madison and Brandeis University. It was in this period that he produced his famous paper on the EPR paradox, from which Bell's theorem could be derived. In 1990, Bell died suddenly from a stroke in Geneva. He was nominated for a Nobel Prize at that time; it was widely expected that he would have won the award if he had lived a few more years. Almost wholly because of Bell's pioneering work, the new field of quantum information theory arose in the 1990s. This includes topics such as quantum cryptography and quantum computing.

ABOUT THE AUTHOR

David Bradshaw is an honorary research fellow at the University of East Anglia in Norwich, UK. He graduated twice from the same university, first receiving a Masters degree in chemical physics (which included a year at the University of Western Ontario, London, Canada) and then a PhD in quantum physics. Overall, David has co-written 87 research papers, all based on quantum electrodynamics. In addition, he has authored four books and acted as volume editor for Elsevier's book 'Comprehensive Nanoscience and Nanotechnology', 2nd edition.

Printed in Great Britain
by Amazon